HOPES
DREAMS
& PROMISE:

THE FUTURE *of* HOMELESS CHILDREN *in* AMERICA

RALPH DaCOSTA NUNEZ

PRESIDENT OF HOMES FOR THE HOMELESS

INTRODUCTION BY

LEONARD N. STERN

FOUNDER OF HOMES FOR THE HOMELESS

Cover and all inside photographs by Todd Flashner
Cover design by Doubling Communications

Published in the United States by
Institute for Children and Poverty
Homes for the Homeless, Inc.
36 Cooper Square, 6th Floor
New York, New York 10003
(212)529-5252

Printed in the United States of America

*This book is dedicated to the children and families
we have served over the years. Their dreams have been
the inspiration for Homes for the Homeless.*

CONTENTS

Preface   xiii

Acknowledgments   xv

Introduction by Leonard N. Stern   1

1.   A New American Poverty: Family Homelessness   11

How Did We Get Here? The Legacy of the 1980s
The First Wave: Housing and Income Changes
Crippling America: Cuts in Social Programs
A Limited Response: Current Homeless Public Policy
Belated and Insufficient Help: Federal Policy
Making Up the Difference Locally: State and Local Initiatives
Homelessness Magnified: The Case of New York City
The Changing Face of Homelessness: New York City Past and Present
A City's Agonizing Dilemma: Homeless Policy in New York City

2. When Is a Shelter Not a Shelter: The Residential   43
    Educational Training Center Model

    The Rationale
        When Shelter is Not Enough: Problems of Traditional Shelters
        An Alternative Approach: Developing Family "Learning Centers"
    The Components
        Putting the Idea to Work: RET Center Operations

3. Breaking the Cycle: Educating the Children   57

    The Rationale
        Unstable Learning: The Effect of Homelessness on Education
        *Creating a New Cycle: Homes for the Homeless Education
            Programs*
    The Components
        A Jump-Start on the Future: Early Childhood Education Programs
        The Learning Fast-track: Accelerated Education Programs
        *Kids Just Want to Have Fun: Recreation and Cultural Programs
            at the Healthy Living Centers*
    The Results: It Can Change

4. Supporting Children by Supporting Parents: 95
    Adult and Family Education

    The Rationale
        *Giving Homeless Families a Chance: Addressing Parental Education
            Needs*
    The Components
        Acquiring the Tools for Success: Adult Education Centers
        Learning the Ropes of Everyday Learning: The PLUS Program
        From Welfare to Work: The Employment Training Program
    The Results
        Alternative High School Results
        PLUS Program Results
        TAG Program Results

5. Keeping Families Together and Healthy: 125
    Prevention and Preservation Programs

    The Rationale
        *Protecting Family Health and Strength: The Need for Prevention and
            Preservation*
    The Components

The Most Essential of Needs: Preventative Health Care Programs
A Necessary But Temporary Separation: The Prospect Family
  Crisis Nursery Program
Bringing Families Together: The Family Reunification and
  Preservation Program
Treating the Family as a Whole: The TIES Program
The Results

6. Moving on to Independent Living: Permanent   153
    Housing Programs

    The Rationale
      Ignoring the Next Step: Post-Shelter Policy and Programs
    The Components
      Mastering the Basics: Permanent Housing Workshops
      Finding a New Home: Housing Placement Programs
      Going the Extra Step: Post-Placement Follow-up Services
    The Results

Conclusion   171

Appendices   175

    I.   *Methodology*
    II. *A History of Homeless Family Rights Litigation in New York*
    III. *RET Center Funding Mechanisms*

Notes   189

Bibliography   225

Index   247

Figures, Tables & Charts

FIGURES

1. *Poverty Rates for Children in the United States 1978-1992*   12

2. *Decrease in HUD Budget Spending for Housing Assistance 1981-1989*   16

3. *The Percentage of All Poor Families Headed by a Single Female 1970-1991*   18

4. *The Change in Federal Spending: Social vs. Military Programs 1980-1990*   19

5. *Median Monthly AFDC Grant for a Family of Three 1970-1992*   21

6. *Decline in the Social Well-Being Index in the United States 1970-1990*   22

7. *The Allocation of McKinney Act Funding by Percent, 1992*   25

8. *McKinney Funds Authorized vs. Funds Appropriated, 1992*   26

9. *Funding Support for Homeless Programs by Level of Government*   27

10. *The Increase in the Number of Homeless Families in New York City 1980-1992* — 30

11. *The Increase in New York City Spending on Homelessness 1982-1993* — 35

12. *Where Homeless Families are Housed in New York City* — 36

13. *Return-to-Homelessness Rates in New York City: Shelters vs. RET Centers* — 48

14. *The Educational Status of Homeless Children vs. Non-Homeless Children* — 63

15. *Percent of Shelters in NYC Offering Educational Services for Children* — 67

16. *Rates of Enrollment in Preschool by Family Income Level* — 71

17. *Developmental Gains of Homeless Children in the Jump-Start Program vs. a Standard Program* — 86

18. *Academic Gains of School-Age Homeless Children in the Brownstone School* — 90

19. *Comparative Daily Attendance Rates for School-Age Children in NYC* — 91

20. *Percentage of Homeless Heads-of-Household with a Substance Abuse Problem* — 128

21. *The Increase in the Foster Care Caseload in New York City 1985-1993* — 130

22. *Why Homeless Families Have an Open Case with Child Welfare Agency* — 133

23. *Events Triggering Use of Family Crisis Nursery* — 142

24. *Homeless Heads-of-Household Receiving Substance Abuse Treatment* — 148

25. *Percent of Homeless Families That Have Lived Independently* — 156

26. *HFH RET Center Sources of Housing Placement for Homeless Families* — 160

27. *Change in PLUS INC Caseload by Need Level - 1989 vs. 1993* — 166

TABLES

1. *Profile of Homeless Heads-of-Household in New York City*   14

2. *Homeless Families - Comparison of 1987 and 1992 Demographics*   32

3. *Comparison of Services in NYC - Emergency Shelters vs. RET
   Center Facilities*   46

4. *Demographic Profile of Homeless School-Aged Children, 1992*   59

5. *Qualifications Needed for Public Assistance Recipients to
   Participate in Job Training Programs vs. the Typical
   Homeless Head-of-Household*   111

6. *Frequency of Childhood Disruptions Among Homeless
   Heads-of-Household*   131

7. *Profile of Homeless Parents with a History of Foster Care vs.
   Parents without a History*   136

8. *Annual Cost of Foster Care Prevention vs. Cost of Foster Care
   Placement, NYC*   151

CHARTS

1. *The RET Center Model*   49

PREFACE

The founders of Homes for the Homeless began with a simple goal: to find a better way to help homeless families in New York City. That was nearly seven years ago, and very few involved had any idea of how much they would learn, how the organization would grow, and, most importantly, how vast a difference we would make in so many lives. Since we opened our first facility in September 1986, we have served more than 7600 families, including 17,300 children, and we have learned a number of important things. First and foremost, homelessness is not simply a housing issue, rather, it is one of children, one of families and one of education. Secondly, the problems these families have are symptomatic of a generation of young Americans growing up in urban poverty and homelessness, in the foster care system and on the street. And, finally, we have learned that there *are* viable solutions and that there is hope for the future. Recognizing that these young families come from backgrounds that include foster care, substance abuse, domestic violence, inadequate health care and poor education has been a driving factor in the creation of all Homes for the Homeless programs and services. In the process of developing, modifying and replicating the best of these programs, we have markedly reduced the number of homeless families in New York City, and believe we have created the blueprint to do so nationally.

This focus on serving the very real problems of urban poverty and homelessness is quite different from the traditional, transitional housing approach that provides families with food and shelter, with minimal counseling and housing placement assistance. From the outset, our service-rich model has taken a much broader approach. We believe that if, during this transition time, families have their dire needs addressed, if they are given the opportunity to gain skills and education, and if parents can learn their critical role in their child's future, we can improve families' lives. Our Residential Educational Training (RET) center model has been created based on these beliefs.

With education being the underlying theme for all our programs, each RET center offers homeless children and their families the chance to break the cycle of poverty and homelessness and gain an independent life. This book, completed in 1993, discusses the realities of homeless children and families in America today: the charts, tables, photographs and words of homeless families contained within these pages demonstrate the severity of this national issue and the grave problems this generation faces. However, we have found that through creativity and commitment, solutions to the daunting problems of urban poverty and homelessness are both possible and affordable. Above all, the story that unfolds is one of hope rather than despair.

December 1993   Ralph da Costa Nunez
New York City

ACKNOWLEDGEMENTS

Hopes, Dreams & Promise is the result of seven years collaboration, experimentation, and vision on the part of numerous friends, staff and organizations associated with Homes for the Homeless.

Our Board of Directors (Reverend James Morton, Leonard N. Stern, Harris Barer, Helaine Barnett, John Brademas, Alexandra Herzan, Carol Kellermann, Sister Joan Kirby, Carol Parry, Charles Persell, Howard Stein, and David Webb) is responsible for having asked the hard questions, and providing us with a vision to face our challenges.

The numerous foundations, corporations and private supporters we have worked with have been our partners in fighting homelessness and poverty. They have provided us with the funding necessary to experiment with innovative programming. Our colleagues at the city, state and federal levels of government have always offered advice and taken our policy and program initiatives seriously.

Thanks to all of the staff at Homes for the Homeless who work, or have worked, with us on the front lines. They deserve credit for the good we have done and all that we have learned. In particular, thanks go to Denise Ingrassia and Aurora Zepeda. We are also grateful to those who have worked so hard on the research and editing of this book: Catherine Kenefick, Laura LoRubbio, Amy Heimerdinger, Randy Pollack, Darcy Seaver, and especially Paige Bartels who masterfully coordinated the overall endeavor. Their energy and patience were indispensable.

Perhaps most importantly, this book would not have been possible without the financial support of two of our collaborators who served as underwriters for this publication. Chemical Bank was instrumental in the founding of Homes for the Homeless by securing our capital financing, contributing to our program funding, and always providing assistance in time of need. They have helped us stay financially healthy and prosperous over the years. In addition, we would like to thank our friends and benefactors, David and Nancy Webb, who have shown their dedication to our mission through their generous support of the Brownstone School and Crisis Nursery programs. David has also committed much time and energy as a board member, and for this we are very grateful. These partnerships are examples of what can be achieved when the public and private sectors join forces.

Lastly, a special thanks to the children and families who shared their stories, impressions, hopes and dreams with us. Their achievements serve as our inspiration.

INTRODUCTION

by Leonard N. Stern

One night in the autumn of 1985, I hosted an out-of-town friend who, during the course of the evening, mentioned that she had never seen lower Manhattan. For me, a lifelong New Yorker, the son of an immigrant, and a businessman, this oversight seemed easy to remedy. So despite the lateness of the hour, we drove downtown for a midnight tour. The most appropriate starting point, I reasoned, would be City Hall.

Who would have guessed that, rather than invigorate me, our visit to this old, imposing center of municipal government would disturb me profoundly, start me on a mission that would alter the way I viewed government, democracy, private enterprise and their impact on the human condition?

We saw eight or nine ragged men that night, all of them asleep, sprawled with their meager possessions in the City Hall park, a tough-looking cop patrolling nearby.

"Why are these people sleeping here, right in front of City Hall?" I asked. "What's going on?"

"Get moving," the officer snapped, planting his hands on his hips to show that he meant business.

I backed away, thought a moment, and then approached him again, this time flashing a press pass from the *Village Voice*. I explained that I owned the New York weekly and suggested that the curious scene might warrant some press attention.

At this point, a strange thing happened: rather than bristle at my challenge or rattle off some official statement, the policeman sighed, allowed his scowl to soften, and looked at me with sorrowful eyes. "Let me tell you what's going on," he said. "The reason they're sleeping down here is that it's safer here than it is at the city homeless shelters."

He began to describe the miserable plight of the "fastest-growing sector of New York City's population," a burgeoning society of displaced people whom he insisted on calling—elliptical as it sounded—"the homeless." Keep in mind that even as late as 1985 this politically correct term had yet to seep into the mainstream. As I viewed it, these people were not "homeless," but were bums, alcoholics, drug users or the mentally disturbed. I'd seen men and women like them my entire life. They were in the Bowery, on park benches, in train stations—all the predictable places. And like anyone who's grown up in an urban environment, I'd become desensitized. But when this soft-spoken policeman estimated the sheer number of destitute people jamming the subway system and overflowing into the parks and streets, and when he described in detail both their crude methods of survival and the violence they faced each night in overrun shelters, I was stunned.

Aware he'd touched a nerve, the officer went on. "Have you ever seen a homeless family?" he asked. "It would break your heart. And the thing about it, it's a hidden problem."

He spoke of young mothers, many of them teenagers, most of them unmarried and uneducated. He described kids who were kicked out of their parents' homes, forced to move, with their babies, from apartment to apartment until the last of their friends or relatives grew tired of them and left them no choice but to seek public shelter. He focused on the homeless children—these children of children—and the emotional damage they suffered. Abandoned by fathers, often neglected by mothers too frazzled or depressed to provide proper care, the children led half-childhoods lain bare by ignorance, abuse, disease and all the other scourges of poverty. He claimed that New York City authorities had set aside the bleakest, most obscure shelters for these homeless women and children, and that, for reasons unknown, both the city and state bureaucracies intentionally kept their numbers quiet...a problem so large, so heartbreaking, that it had to be hidden from public view!

Troubled by what I'd heard that night, I made it my business to observe and investigate this tragedy for myself.

Although New York State prohibits private citizens from entering the shelters used to house homeless families, I eventually found my way up to the Roberto Clemente Housing Project in the Bronx and managed to gain entry to its basement, which was reserved exclusively for homeless families. You should understand that never in my life—a life grounded in the belief that the American system ensures, above all, the innocence of children and their right to pursue the boldest of dreams—have I encountered anything so shocking, so beyond comprehension. It shook the very foundations upon which my immigrant father and I had raised our families. This simply could not be happening in my America!

This place was horrendous. The huge, dimly lit, stripped-down gymnasium contained about 400 cots grouped together in family sets along the open floor. There were no lockers. Each family kept their possessions in plastic garbage bags beneath their cots. Needless to say, from the moment the shelter opened at five in the evening until its mandatory "close-out" at 10 the next morning, nobody strayed far from their designated area. Anyone who wished to leave, for whatever reason, was forced to check out with the one social worker on site—with their children and all their personal belongings—and then check back in upon their return. In our midst were a number of armed policemen who stood stiffly against the walls, stirring now and then to brush back an unruly child or bark instructions to a confused mother. Policemen also monitored the communal bathrooms, with young boys over the age of five required to use the "men's only" facilities under the watchful eye of a state trooper. This mass of dejected humanity was something I would never forget.

I walked among the cots and children surrounded me, playing and having fun the way kids seem to do no matter what the circumstance. I couldn't help but smile. Nearby a confused-looking little girl sat in the lap of a well-dressed woman who sobbed, her face in her hands. I sat down and asked if she wanted to discuss what had happened. She explained that she, her husband and her daughter were taking a trip. During a layover at John F. Kennedy airport, her husband ran off with all of their money and possessions. Eventually she had landed at the shelter, where she'd have to stay until she figured things out. During the course of our conversation, she mentioned that she was a college graduate. Another woman, equally articulate, told me she'd lost everything in a fire. She confided that she and her two kids had worn the same clothes for nearly a week.

Not all of the stories I heard that evening were so exceptional, but every woman shared the same predicament: they were young, single mothers with nowhere to go but this dirty, impersonal place. On my way home that night, I decided to do something about it. I called my old friend Helaine Barnett, Deputy Attorney in Charge at The Legal Aid Society, and pledged $1 million to the organization's Homeless Family Rights Project—a project that sought to establish and enforce minimum legal entitlements for homeless families.

That same week I returned to City Hall. This time I met with then-Mayor Koch, related what I'd heard and seen, and asked him to explain the city's side of the story. He spoke candidly about the situation, with sincere compassion in his voice. Frustrated, he listed for me all the reasons why the city could not improve the conditions for these people. And I believed him, recognized that he was a prisoner to his own bureaucratic system. "If I can come up with the answers to some of the problems," I asked, "will you support my efforts?" "If you can manage that," he said, "I'll do everything I can to help."

"You'll hear from me," I promised.

Shortly thereafter, at a news conference announcing my $1 million dollar gift to Legal Aid, I expounded on my ideas and then detailed them in a *New York Times* op-ed piece. The day after it appeared in the newspaper, I received a call from New York Governor Mario Cuomo. He'd read my editorial in the *Times* and expressed interest in working together as soon as possible. His Housing Commissioner, William Emmett, arrived at my home within the hour. After a long discussion, we reached an agreement, if not on the methods then at least on the need for reform.

For the next few nights, I visited numerous welfare hotels, shelters and Emergency Assistance Units (EAU's). (Homeless families in New York City must first go to a city-operated EAU, where they must register before going to a shelter in one of the five boroughs. By law, the city must find them a place to sleep within 24 hours.) One evening at an EAU in the Bronx, I sat silently and watched as dozens of haggard mothers, many of them holding sleeping babies or dozing off themselves, were called up to booths staffed by government workers. The clerks asked the women a few questions, investigated the children for measles and other contagious diseases and then offered them shelter placement for the night. Around midnight I spotted a woman trudging up to an interview booth alone. She looked like she'd been waiting all day. I overheard the clerk ask her where her children were, and she said they were sleeping with friends in another borough. The clerk refused to assign her a place until she retrieved her kids. When the woman started to cry, the clerk toughened up and motioned for an armed officer to remove her. I jumped up and shouted, "That's enough!" Then another officer appeared and threatened to arrest me if I didn't leave.

Out of nowhere, a man stepped forward and introduced himself as an official from the governor's office. Things quieted down and the man and I sat and traded observations. "No one was aware how extreme the problems are for these families," he maintained. I reasserted how much I wanted to do something. But at this point, I confess, I wasn't sure where to begin.

Ben Holloway, then Chairman of Equitable Insurance Real Estate Division, suggested that I join forces with the Cathedral of St. John the Divine, which has a long history of dedication to the plight of the urban poor in New York City. On his advice I met with the head of the Cathedral, the Very Reverend James Parks Morton, and suggested in broad terms what I felt needed to be done. Together we organized a conference of representatives from city, state, and local non-profit organizations. I promised that if they conceived a model for an organization to help homeless families, I'd make things happen. I'd finance it. And after they came through with a viable model, I presented it to the mayor as a joint proposal, one that would enlist both the private and public sectors. I must say that no one cooperated more during the program's early stages of development than Mayor Koch and his Deputy Mayor, Stanley Brezenoff. The unlikely three-way partnership between government, private enterprise and the non-profit sector worked smoothly. This partnership enabled the original $200,000 I advanced for the first Homes for the Homeless facility to evolve into an organization that is now the largest single provider of transitional housing and services for homeless families in New York City. For the next six years, the Hartz Mountain Corporation–of which I am Chairman—continued to make substantial contributions, as well as extending more than $20 million in financing guarantees to enable Homes for the Homeless to acquire its facilities.

Over the years, we've proven a few things. In the process of serving over 7600 families, including over 17,300 children, we've shown how three separate entities, (the private sector, the public sector and the non-profit sector) with three different agendas, can combine their best efforts to achieve a singular goal, a goal that no one could achieve alone. Our program's success in this huge, difficult urban environment, as well as its social effectiveness and economic efficiency, will, I hope, inspire other local governments to replicate our model and end the cycle of family homelessness.

We never imagined when we began that we'd make such a difference in so many lives. The story of Homes for the Homeless must be told not only to show what has been done, but also to stir readers to reconsider their own attitudes towards this fragile society of people. The majority of the homeless are not, as many believe, erratic, mentally disturbed males; rather, 75 percent of the homeless in New York City are families and children. They are victims of poverty, often unemployed mothers and their children. They are poor people. And in an affluent free-enterprise society, there is a deep prejudice against the poor—they are somehow blamed for their indigence. People seek easy explanations and ignore outside factors: "Look at that lazy woman," they say, "she'll be on welfare forever." But we must remember that the children are the real victims and that society is indeed responsible for their welfare.

Many may ask when they see an abandoned mother with an infant, or with three young children, "Why doesn't she work?" And I say that a young, single mother with an infant and other small children who has fought to keep her family together, who has resisted giving up her children to foster care, is working. Even if you don't agree with me, I ask, "Are the children to blame?" You must keep in mind that throughout it all, these mothers face enormous pressure each day to give up their children to foster care—an easy escape in many respects. Instead, most of these women make tremendous sacrifices to keep their children. Nonetheless, the stigma of being a poor mother remains. At Homes for the Homeless we try, above all, to deflect this ingrained prejudice from the children, to preserve their innocence, and to promote their growth by providing them and their mothers with a stable and healthy environment, as well as educational opportunities.

My involvement with Homes for the Homeless has, perhaps more than anything, deepened my understanding of democratic government and made me aware of how delicately the entire system lies in balance. For democracy to really work, the promise of equal opportunity must be tempered with built-in safeguards so that the most vulnerable members of the system are not excluded. Failing to insure the basic principles of fairness and civil rights erodes the very foundation of our political system. Thankfully, it has been my impression that, when those in government or industry sees for themselves the tender young lives that are at stake, their desire to help comes naturally. And when one sees how easily Homes for the Homeless helped so many, it is my hope that others all over this great and rich country will use our model to make a difference in their own communities.

Kelly, Carrie and Christopher
1993

A
NEW AMERICAN
POVERTY:

Family Homelessness

Poverty has become a fixture of the American landscape. Although we all have opinions about its causes and effects, few of us can offer viable solutions. We shake our heads at poverty statistics and feel frustrated and threatened by its manifestations: unemployment, crime, violence, drug abuse. We cope by numbing ourselves to poverty's scourge, even as it tears at our nation's social fabric.

Sadly, poverty has claimed America's children as its greatest victims. In only 10 years, the number of children living below the poverty line has increased nationwide by nearly 25 percent. The number of poor children soared by more than three million in the 1980s, outpacing the overall population growth of children in the United States. By 1992, *one in every four* children under the age of six was poor (see Figure 1). Children in cities face even harsher odds: nearly one-third will grow up in poverty. Overall, the child poverty rate in this country is now at least double that of other "developed" nations.[1]

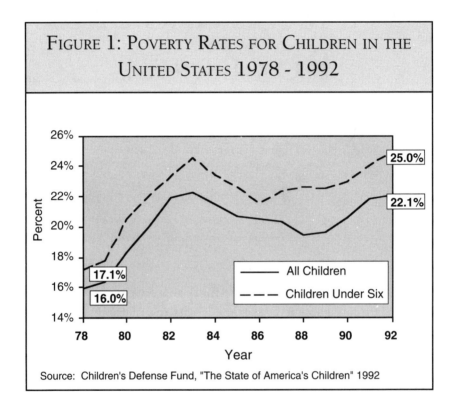

FIGURE 1: POVERTY RATES FOR CHILDREN IN THE UNITED STATES 1978 - 1992

Source: Children's Defense Fund, "The State of America's Children" 1992

The percentage of children living below the poverty line increased nearly 25 percent since 1980.

In these poverty statistics looms a tragic phenomenon familiar to more and more poor children: homelessness. A term synonymous with poverty, homelessness began drawing national attention in the early 1980s. Although many Americans today assume that homelessness is principally a plight of transient individuals, in fact, the fastest growing group of homeless is families with children. In several U.S. cities, including New York, families make up over half of the homeless population. Some experts estimate that the annual number of homeless children in the United States may be as high as two million. If such estimates are accurate, their numbers compare to the entire population of the city of Miami.[2]

However, these families and their children are more than simply homeless. They also lack adequate education, health care and job skills. Indeed, these factors best explain *why* most families are homeless. Today's homeless families tend to be headed by very young women raising their children on their own, usually without any form of child support from absent fathers. Most have less than a high school education and little, if any, work experience. They are often grappling with problems of domestic violence, substance abuse and poor health. And most have few people to turn to for help: one of the most consistent differences between homeless and non-homeless families is that the former tend to lack even basic social supports such as nearby family members or community ties. Frequently, just out of a disruptive foster-care system themselves, or fleeing abusive partners, these young mothers are desperately on their own (see Table 1).[3]

Such problems are interrelated and most are common to poor people. And while homeless families represent an especially severe and troubling form of poverty, it is important to remember the *majority* of poor families, not just homeless families, are led by young, single women with inadequate educations, work experience and support networks. These young parents, many of whom grew up poor themselves, face an almost impossible challenge: they must provide child

TABLE 1: PROFILE OF HOMELESS HEADS-OF-HOUSEHOLD IN NEW YORK CITY

Characteristics	1992
Gender	
Female	97%
Single	87%
Married	13%
Average Age (yrs)	22
Under 25 years	56%
25 years and Over	44%
Education History	
High School or GED Graduate	37%
Not a High School Graduate	63%
Employment History	
Have Work Experience	70%
Have Held a Job for Over 6 Months	40%
Currently Working	3%
Have Never Worked	30%
Social Welfare Indicators	
Substance Abuse History	71%
Domestic Violence History	43%
Mental Illness History	10%
Pregnant/Recently Gave Birth	49%
In Foster Care as a Child	20%

Source: Institute for Children and Poverty

Today the typical homeless family head-of-household is a young, single woman without a high school diploma or substantial work experience. There is a 50 percent chance that she is currently pregnant. She has most likely experienced substance abuse and is probably the victim of domestic violence and perhaps has lived in foster care as a child.

care and find a job that will support the entire family with few means to accomplish either. They are limited to low-paying, low-skill jobs that can barely bring their families above the poverty line, let alone provide child care, health care and decent housing. Existing government programs offer little help in overcoming or preventing this quandary. As a result, most poor families today—and their children's families tomorrow—will remain trapped in poverty.[4]

For the growing number of homeless families, the outlook is bleaker still. They face even greater barriers than other poor Americans do when it comes to acquiring the education and resources needed to escape poverty. Housing alone does not resolve the interconnected problems such families battle, nor does it ensure them a future without poverty. In fact, as long as such issues go unaddressed, these families stand at risk of repeated episodes of homelessness. A young mother unqualified for the job that would lift her family out of poverty remains without the necessary tools for success even as she moves into a new home. Domestic violence is as destructive to a family's well-being and future in a house as it is in a shelter. And a child growing up in an apartment without solid education, health care or support will still likely confront a lifetime of poverty.

HOW DID WE GET HERE? THE LEGACY OF THE 1980s

The U.S. homeless population was expanding as early as the 1960s, but nothing since the Great Depression compares to the surge that took place in the 1980s. Changes in the job and housing markets account for some of the increase, but perhaps most important was the systematic dismantling of the "safety net" that had long supported the nation's poor and disadvantaged. The funding cuts initiated by the Reagan and Bush Administrations resulted in the loss of programs that had both prevented and broken the cycle of poverty. Without them, the cycle became only more endemic and complex. By the end of the decade, the policies of the 1980s had bequeathed to the nation not only a crippling economic deficit, but a social one as well.[5]

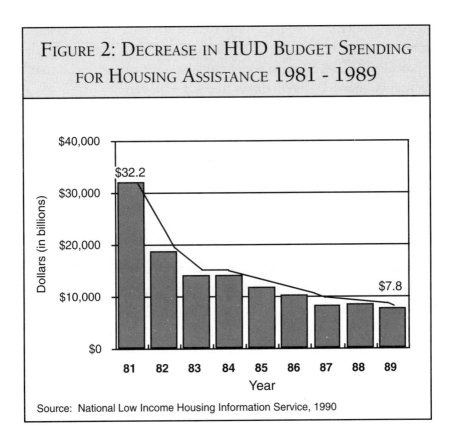

FIGURE 2: DECREASE IN HUD BUDGET SPENDING FOR HOUSING ASSISTANCE 1981 - 1989

Source: National Low Income Housing Information Service, 1990

Over the last decade, federal spending for housing assistance decreased by 78 percent.

The First Wave: Housing and Income Changes

In the 1960s and 1970s, the number of homeless Americans began to increase gradually in the wake of a series of public policy shifts. Most significant were those affecting the availability of low-income housing and the treatment of the mentally ill. As the number of single-occupancy housing units decreased, along with public housing subsidies, and as growing numbers of mentally ill people were discharged from public institutions without adequate housing or services in communities, the homeless population in many cities swelled. However, most of the new homeless during this period were single adults.[6]

In 1981, with a new Administration in Washington, the face of homelessness began to change. On one level, this was because the housing trends of the past 15 years were simply made worse: the stock of low-income housing decreased still further as public housing programs and subsidies were slashed by more than 75 percent (see Figure 2). Existing low-income housing aged, was gentrified, or deteriorated and, overall, housing prices increased. At the same time, the economy stagnated and unemployment soared, particularly in those manufacturing sectors that had traditionally employed unskilled or low-skilled workers. Income levels for female-headed families fell more sharply than those of any other group and the poverty rate for those families increased dramatically (see Figure 3). As a result, fewer people in general, and even fewer families headed by women, could find or afford housing.[7]

Crippling America: Cuts in Social Programs

It was the contraction in national social spending during this period, however, that broadened and deepened the problem of homelessness. Beginning with President Ronald Reagan's Omnibus Budget Reconciliation Act of 1981, federal funding for a vast array of social programs was slashed or capped, a process that soon resonated at all levels of government and community (see Figure 4).

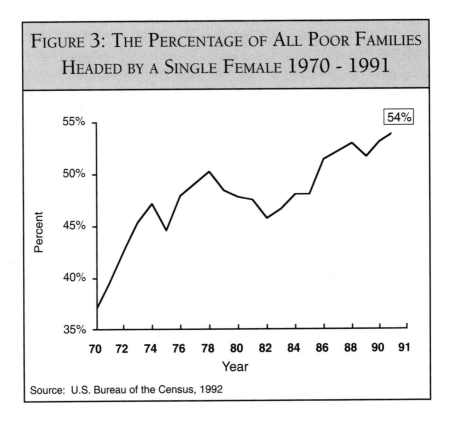

FIGURE 3: THE PERCENTAGE OF ALL POOR FAMILIES HEADED BY A SINGLE FEMALE 1970 - 1991

Source: U.S. Bureau of the Census, 1992

Since 1970, there has been a 46 percent increase in the number of poor families headed by a single female.

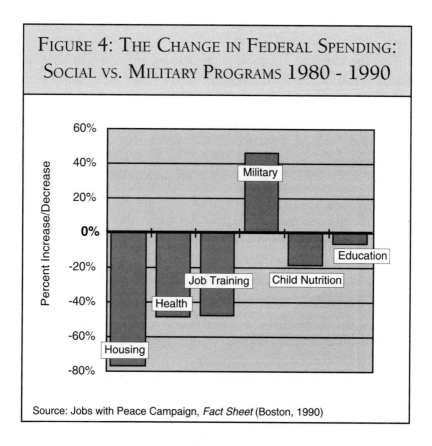

FIGURE 4: THE CHANGE IN FEDERAL SPENDING: SOCIAL VS. MILITARY PROGRAMS 1980 - 1990

Source: Jobs with Peace Campaign, *Fact Sheet* (Boston, 1990)

Federal spending for all social programs, particularly those benefiting poor children, was significantly reduced throughout the 1980s.

Included in the cuts were programs that helped low-income families avoid the worst ravages of poverty, such as AFDC (Aid to Families with Dependent Children), where the government sliced benefits and raised eligibility levels (see Figure 5). The administration cut billions of dollars from the Food Stamp Program, driving one million recipients off the program, even as more Americans were sinking into poverty. Most of those who were denied benefits were children.[8]

Equally damaging were cuts to programs that had historically worked to prevent or limit poverty, namely education programs. In the 1980s federal support for elementary and secondary education dropped by *one-third*. Hardest hit were those areas most in need—poorer districts with insufficient property-tax revenues to make up the difference in lost federal monies. As a result, poor children today attend the worst schools, are lost in larger classes and are taught by less-qualified teachers than their peers in more affluent areas. Higher dropout rates and poorer achievement levels among low-income children attest to these disparities.[9]

Other critical services and supports also evaporated. Programs around the country were forced to curtail or even abandon their efforts to prevent and treat the problems so decried and troubling today, including drug abuse, teenage pregnancy and domestic violence. As the problems worsened at each level of society, all Americans suffered (see Figure 6). But the problems of the poor were particularly aggravated. Unlike those who could afford alternative private programs, low-income people were left largely on their own to fight the very problems that exacerbate and perpetuate the state of poverty. Moreover, increasing numbers of people became poor as drugs ravaged neighborhoods and the unmarried teen birth rate skyrocketed.[10]

Even more tragic was an especially harsh form of poverty now swallowing more and more American parents and children. These families were facing problems and deprivations that amounted, and

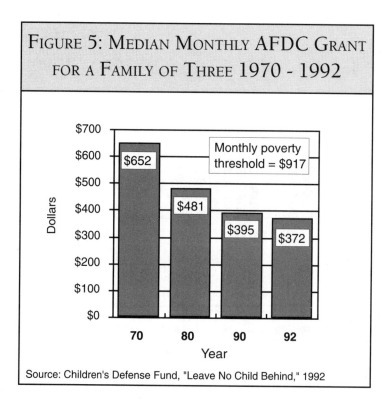

FIGURE 5: MEDIAN MONTHLY AFDC GRANT FOR A FAMILY OF THREE 1970 - 1992

Source: Children's Defense Fund, "Leave No Child Behind," 1992

Since 1970, the median monthly AFDC (Aid to Families with Dependent Children) grant was reduced by 43 percent, and is still substantially below the poverty threshold.

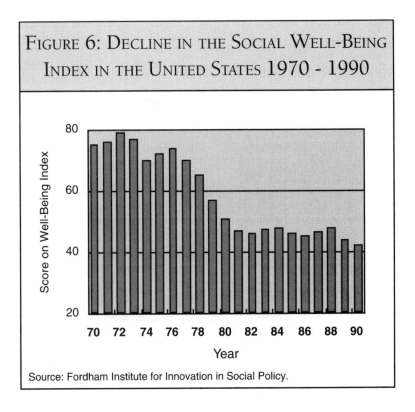

FIGURE 6: DECLINE IN THE SOCIAL WELL-BEING INDEX IN THE UNITED STATES 1970 - 1990

Source: Fordham Institute for Innovation in Social Policy.

The social well-being in the United States, as measured by an index of significant social indicators, including such problems as poverty, teen suicide, child abuse, drug abuse and drop-out rates, has shown a marked decrease in the past decade.

continue to amount to, virtual disenfranchisement. This "underclass" was even poorer, less educated and less equipped than other low-income families to overcome the economic and housing challenges of this period. So they fell farther and farther into poverty, as the income support and social services they needed most desperately of all, including education, disappeared or deteriorated. *And they became homeless in record numbers.* It is these families, the poorest of the poor, who have swelled the ranks of America's homeless since the 1980s and who have broadened the issue of homelessness far beyond housing.

A LIMITED RESPONSE: CURRENT HOMELESS PUBLIC POLICY

These policies begin to explain why we have more poor and homeless Americans today than ever before, and why their problems are so complex. The 1980s were devastating on this score. Today's policies, however, remain inadequate. No truly comprehensive national policy exists to address either homelessness or poverty. Meanwhile, state and local initiatives are hobbled by fiscal limitations and short-sighted solutions. Subsequently, most have failed, as evidenced by the annually increasing numbers of homeless families and children.

Belated and Insufficient Help: Federal Policy

Despite the growing numbers in the early 1980s, the federal government continued to rely on a piecemeal and short-term approach to the problem of homelessness. Finally, in 1987, when the number of homeless people in the United States had doubled in less than five years, Congress enacted the primary legislation still guiding federal policy today: The Stewart B. McKinney Homelessness Assistance Act.[11]

The McKinney Act currently allocates $945.9 million for over 20 programs that assist the homeless. Most of this money is tagged for "urgent needs" such as shelter, food and health care. Only a very small portion goes to other programs essential to overcoming homelessness, such as education and job training (see Figure 7).

Moreover, McKinney allots a disproportionate amount of funding to programs for the single adult homeless population, shortchanging the more rapidly growing numbers of homeless children and families.[12]

The McKinney Act is flawed in other ways as well. First, it has left the use of federal funds primarily to the discretion of individual states, but has allocated this funding in fragments drawn from separate programs and tied to very specific services. As a result, states have had difficulties devising comprehensive, coordinated approaches to the complex problems of homelessness. The lack of focus has also been evident on the federal level, for despite the fundamental link between homelessness and poverty, there has been little coordination between homeless programs and the welfare system.[13]

Administrative and funding problems have also impaired the federal programs. Under past administrations, McKinney Act grants were typically awarded based on state matching funds. Yet, with overall federal aid steadily dwindling and their local tax bases constricted by a troubled national economy, states have been hard pressed to find the money to qualify them for grants. As a result, funds have frequently gone unappropriated and service needs unmet (see Figure 8). Furthermore, a lack of coordination between the federal and local levels of government means that many programs have been poorly implemented or insufficiently monitored.[14]

Making Up the Difference Locally: State and Local Initiatives

With limited federal aid and direction, homelessness has become a local and community responsibility. Many states and municipalities have devoted significant portions of their budgets each year to the problem (see Figure 9). They scramble to handle, with shrinking funds, what amounts to an expanding emergency. They respond from a crisis perspective with the primary focus on providing emergency shelter and meeting immediate needs.[15]

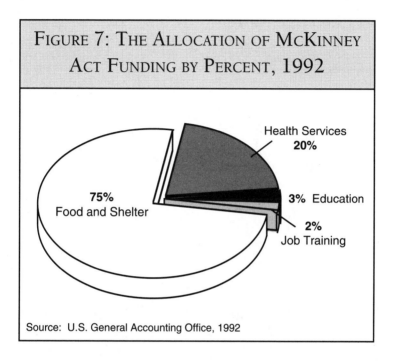

FIGURE 7: THE ALLOCATION OF MCKINNEY ACT FUNDING BY PERCENT, 1992

Health Services
20%

75%
Food and Shelter

3% Education

2%
Job Training

Source: U.S. General Accounting Office, 1992

Three quarters of all McKinney monies for the homeless are spent on simply providing emergency services, such as food and shelter. A relatively small percent goes to other programs, such as education and job training, that are essential to overcoming homelessness.

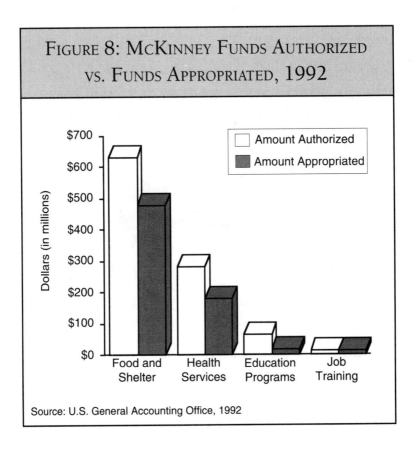

FIGURE 8: McKINNEY FUNDS AUTHORIZED
vs. FUNDS APPROPRIATED, 1992

Source: U.S. General Accounting Office, 1992

McKinney funds are typically awarded based on state matching grants. However, with states hard pressed to find the funds needed to qualify them for such grants, the McKinney dollars authorized by Congress are significantly greater than those actually appropriated.

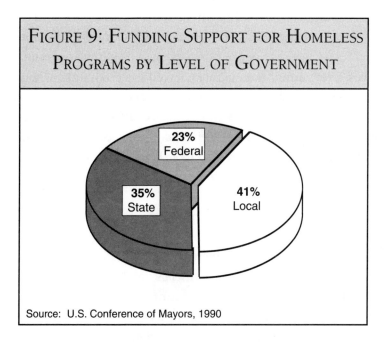

FIGURE 9: FUNDING SUPPORT FOR HOMELESS
PROGRAMS BY LEVEL OF GOVERNMENT

23%
Federal

35%
State

41%
Local

Source: U.S. Conference of Mayors, 1990

With limited Federal aid and an increasing need for programs to serve the homeless, the bulk of the weight for funding such programs has fallen on the shoulders of local governments.

Most state-level homeless policy has been shaped by government task forces, comprised of various state, local and private agencies. For the most part, however, the task forces serve merely as information-sharing bodies with no power to mandate. And even when such task forces are able to go beyond an emergency response, they tend to view the problem of homelessness too narrowly. Housing becomes the central focus, at the expense of needs such as education and family services. Every administrator interviewed in a 1988 study of homeless programs in California, Connecticut, Georgia, New Mexico, Ohio and Wisconsin reported that they saw the lack of affordable housing as the main factor in the creation and perpetuation of homelessness. Consequently, most states have focused on creating more housing, without the support or transitional services needed to equip families to remain in this housing.[16]

Given their constraints—both fiscal and political—it is not surprising that state and local responses have generally failed to make substantial progress. Recent studies illuminate the inadequate, and at times detrimental, government response. Officials in 70 percent of the cities surveyed in 1992 by the U.S. Conference of Mayors claimed state budget cuts had increased local homeless populations. The same study also found that homeless families are particularly underserved. In more than 75 percent of the participating cities, homeless families made up the largest group for whom shelter and services were most seriously lacking.[17]

HOMELESSNESS MAGNIFIED: THE CASE OF NEW YORK CITY

New York City provides an instructive glimpse both at the way homelessness is progressing and the change in response to it. As is true in many cities, New York's homeless population has changed dramatically over the past 10 years, not only in size but in composition. Moreover, it continues to evolve, as a new generation of homeless families emerges with its own set of problems and needs. The city has poured millions of local dollars into a sprawling, inefficient shelter system that is criticized and resisted on all fronts, even by city officials. Yet there is also hope, much of it based on reforming and enriching key components of that same shelter system, particularly its transitional housing facilities. The Homes for the Homeless (HFH) model of Residential Educational Training (RET) centers, developed over the last seven years, offers one of the most promising strategies for this transformation.

The Changing Face of Homelessness: New York City Past and Present

Although the population of single homeless adults in New York City gradually increased in the 1970s, as was true across the country, the number of homeless families held relatively constant throughout the decade. Up to that time, an average of 940 families per year lived in the city's emergency shelters. For most of these families homelessness was simply a temporary displacement resulting from fire, illness or some short-term financial crisis.[18]

However, in the early 1980s, a dramatic change took place as the Reagan Administration's reduction of social programs and aid to cities began to take effect. Between 1982 and 1983, the number of homeless families surged from less than 1000 to over 2400. Reflecting national trends, their numbers had climbed still higher by 1988, reaching an unprecedented 5200 families. In less than one decade New York had witnessed an astounding *500 percent* increase in the number of families confronting homelessness (see Figure 10).[19]

Today, nearly 6000 homeless families live in the city's shelter system, including roughly 11,000 children. Every month, 1000 new families seek help. By 1994, entrenched poverty and a continued dearth of desperately needed services are expected to drive those numbers up another 30 percent or more, to a record 13,000 children and their 8000 families.[20]

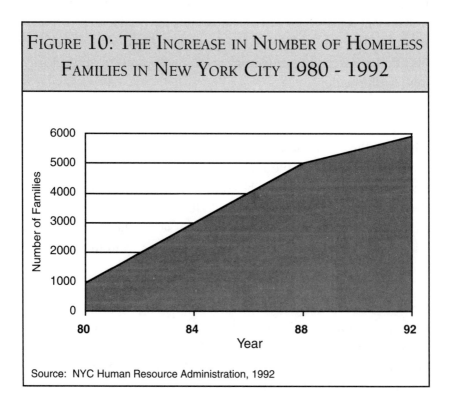

FIGURE 10: THE INCREASE IN NUMBER OF HOMELESS FAMILIES IN NEW YORK CITY 1980 - 1992

Source: NYC Human Resource Administration, 1992

After remaining relatively constant for over a decade, the number of homeless families increased dramatically beginning in 1982. By 1992, there were close to 6000 homeless families living in New York City shelters—a 500 percent increase in only 10 years.

There have also been striking changes in the characteristics of New York City's homeless families over the last 10 years. Although no comparative city-wide or national information is available, Homes for the Homeless has been collecting data that constitutes a representative sample of the city's homeless population. This demographic data illustrates the fundamental shifts that have occurred.

First, families have become younger. Where even five years ago a 35-year-old woman headed the typical homeless family entering an HFH RET Center, today that responsibility falls most commonly to a woman younger than 22 years old. Her children are significantly younger, too. Today, 80 percent of homeless children are younger than age six, whereas only 15 percent fell into this bracket five years ago (see Table 2).[21]

Not surprisingly, these young heads-of-household tend to have less education and work experience. Five years ago, more than half of the heads-of-households were high school graduates. Today, only 37 percent have graduated. Furthermore, less than half (40 percent) of all family heads have even six months of employment experience; five years ago some 60 percent could claim that amount.

If today's homeless head-of-household is more often undereducated and lacking job skills, she is also more likely to be unmarried and raising her children alone. Five years ago, a full 92 percent of homeless families at HFH were headed by single women. Today, virtually *all* are. And, as young as they are, these women are usually raising entire families with no experience in living independently. By 1992, nearly half of the families coming to HFH had never lived in their own apartment. Better than three-fourths had been "doubled up"—living temporarily with friends or relatives. More than ever before, homeless heads-of-household are coming directly from childhood—often via the foster care system—to parenthood on the streets.

TABLE 2: HOMELESS FAMILIES – COMPARISON OF 1987 AND 1992 DEMOGRAPHICS		
Characteristics	1987	1992
Gender		
Female	92%	97%
Single	60%	87%
Married	40%	13%
Average Age (yrs)	35	22
Under 25 years	27%	56%
25 years and Over	73%	44%
Education History		
High School or GED Graduate	62%	37%
Not a High School Graduate	38%	63%
Employment History		
Have Held a Job for Over 6 Months	60%	40%
Have Held a Job for Over 1 Year	36%	21%
Social Welfare Indicators		
Substance Abuse History	23%	71%
Domestic Violence History	32%	43%
Pregnant/Recently Had Baby	15%	49%
In Foster Care as a Child	5%	20%
Source: Institute for Children and Poverty		

By 1992, the typical profile of a homeless family had changed significantly. Today we are faced with a new generation of homeless families with more chronic conditions of poverty than just half a decade ago.

HFH has also identified striking changes in the severity and breadth of problems now engulfing homeless families. One of the most debilitating problems is substance abuse, which has risen precipitously over the last five years among these women. In 1987, 23 percent of homeless family heads had histories of drug and alcohol abuse. Half a decade later, more than three times as many—71 percent—struggle with such problems.

Domestic violence is also more common. Today nearly half of all HFH clients report a history of family violence, where less than a third did five years ago. One in 10 has lived temporarily in a battered women's shelter. Even more telling, 20 percent of today's families cite violence in the home as the primary cause of their homelessness. Nor does the problem stand alone: more than a third of HFH clients report that in their families, domestic violence and substance abuse are interrelated problems.

Not surprisingly, children growing up homeless today tend to suffer from more than just a lack of housing. Inadequate health care is one of the most obvious problems. In addition to receiving insufficient immunizations, homeless children experience upper-respiratory infections and gastrointestinal, ear and dermatological disorders at more than *double* the rate of other low-income children. Even before these children are born they often lack critical medical care. Although nearly half of all women in HFH's RET centers are either currently pregnant or caring for newborn babies, 33 percent have never received any prenatal care. And although difficult to quantify, anecdotal information suggests that even when prenatal care is obtained, it is sporadic and usually initiated late in the pregnancy. This may very well be the norm, since overall, the infant mortality rate among New York City's homeless is more than *double* that of the city's general population.[22]

As the following chapters show, homeless children confront many other challenges. They desperately lack educational opportunities and support. They are often the victims of abuse, neglect and malnutrition. They risk being absorbed into destructive cycles of underachievement and abuse, to say nothing of poverty itself. As their needs have intensified and their problems have grown more severe over the past decade, homeless children and their families require new, more comprehensive support and services, such as those offered at HFH's RET centers. As the following discussion of New York City policy suggests, revamping the current system to meet these needs is a challenge, but one that is both manageable and desperately needed.

A City's Agonizing Dilemma: Homeless Policy in New York City

As New York City watched its homeless population soar in the 1980s and early '90s, it did not fail to respond. Every year, the city devoted more and more funds to the crisis, even as federal monies were disappearing. Between 1978 and 1985 alone, the city's budget allocation for emergency shelters rose from $8 million to over $100 million (see Figure 11). It expanded the number of shelters, opened specialized facilities and attempted to provide shelter to all homeless people. By 1988, it was devoting more local funds to homelessness than any other municipality in the country. Today, the city devotes over $400 million to shelter operations alone.[23]

Yet virtually everyone—including Mayor David N. Dinkins—agrees that the New York City shelter system has been inadequate. It is still widely regarded as fragmented, wasteful and, in some cases, even dangerous. This is not entirely the city's fault; like municipalities across the nation, New York has faced severe fiscal constraints and, as a government body, tends to focus primarily on the emergency dimensions of the problem: providing temporary shelter, rather than broad-based crucial services.[24]

As the system is structured today, a "shelter" in New York City refers to three types of facilities. One is the ubiquitous "welfare hotel." Made notorious in the 1980s, when they housed the great majority of

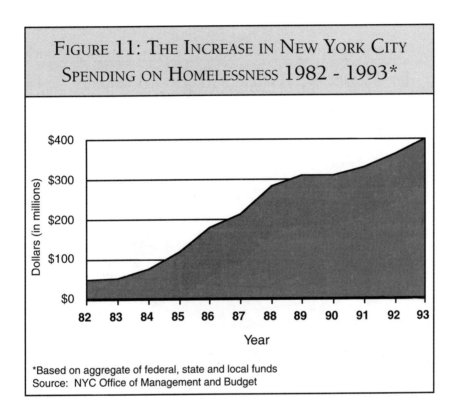

FIGURE 11: THE INCREASE IN NEW YORK CITY
SPENDING ON HOMELESSNESS 1982 - 1993*

*Based on aggregate of federal, state and local funds
Source: NYC Office of Management and Budget

*Despite its persistent financial problems, New York City devotes more
local funds to homelessness than any other municipality in the country. In 1992,
New York City allocated over $400 million dollars to its shelter operations.*

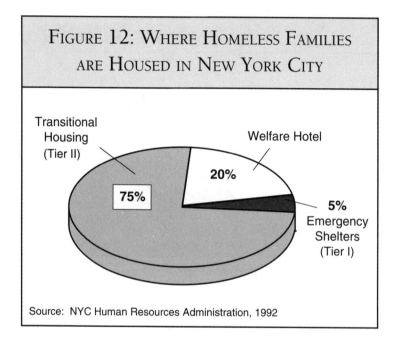

FIGURE 12: WHERE HOMELESS FAMILIES ARE HOUSED IN NEW YORK CITY

Transitional Housing (Tier II)

Welfare Hotel

20%

75%

5% Emergency Shelters (Tier I)

Source: NYC Human Resources Administration, 1992

With the majority of New York City's homeless families residing in transitional housing facilities (Tier II's), the opportunity to provide services that will reduce their depth of poverty has never been greater.

New York's homeless, the hotels are still known for their squalid, overcrowded conditions and wasteful costs. Nonetheless, the city continues to rely on them to house roughly 20 percent of today's homeless families (see Figure 12). At a hotel a family typically stays in one room with either private or shared bathroom facilities. Few services, if any, are available.[25]

A second type of city shelter is the "Tier I" emergency facility, usually a large congregate building, such as a school gymnasium or military armory, where numerous families or single adults are put up barracks-style overnight. The city has reduced the use of these facilities in the past several years in response to both legal mandates and harsh criticism of their crowded and unsafe conditions (for further discussion of the litigation surrounding homelessness, see Appendix II, A Legal History of Homelessness, prepared by the Legal Aid Society of New York). Still, it continues to use them for approximately 5 percent of the system's homeless families. Tier I's provide minimal services, even those as basic as housing assistance and medical attention. The little counseling available is stretched thin, as caseworkers struggle to assist as many as 60 families each. And providing education to children living in such facilities is extremely difficult, as the Board of Education often loses track of them as they are shuffled from one shelter to another.[26]

Today the most commonly used family shelter is the "Tier II" transitional facility, which houses about 75 percent of New York City's homeless families. Developed in response to the criticisms of emergency shelters, these apartment-style facilities function as transitional housing rather than merely overnight shelter. Tier II's offer more privacy and are mandated by state regulations to maintain a limited threshold of services including counseling, housing assistance and recreation. Families typically live at Tier II's for extended periods as they prepare for the transition to permanent housing.

Clinton RET Center

1993

"Getting past the Emergency Assistance Unit is the hardest part," says 24 year-old Anna, a Clinton Residential Educational Training center resident. "It's so filthy and scary that you think wherever you're going to be sent to live will be the same way. So it's a big relief when you're sent to a nice, clean place."

Anna, mother of a two-year-old daughter, describes her experiences living at the Clinton. She has gained the self-esteem to overlook the stigmas of homelessness, to foster friendships with other residents and to take part in programs that help her become independent. "This place is definitely different. I've grown, I've gained, I've matured. I've become more responsible, and I have the people here to thank for much of that."

All three types of shelter were developed for short-term stays, as "way stations" in the search for permanent housing. However, in practice, they often represent endurance tests as families find themselves waiting sometimes as long as several years for an apartment. That wait often takes place in strange and unfamiliar surroundings as the shelter system places families arbitrarily, frequently with the consequence of removing homeless people from their neighborhoods, thereby further isolating already vulnerable, young families. Even when available, support and services are generally fragmented and temporary. And more often than not, a homeless family has no one contact person or caseworker to turn to during their ordeal.[27]

The failure of this system has been all too apparent. Even with city government spending at an all-time high, New York City's homeless problem is as bad as ever and continues to worsen. Although much of this relates to larger problems in the economy and in housing markets, it is also the consequence of defining homelessness too narrowly. Until now, New York City has approached homelessness as primarily a problem of insufficient housing. Consequently, it has focused on providing that housing, first through temporary shelter and then through placement in permanent homes. But this response has failed miserably, mainly because it ignores today's reality: lack of housing is no longer the primary issue behind most homelessness.

As HFH and others documenting the changes in New York City family homelessness have found, families are homeless today not so much because of a lack of housing but because of inadequate family resources. They are unable to provide for themselves because of a lack of education, independent living skills, social supports and family problems. This is why housing alone is not the solution, and why those programs that go beyond housing have shown the most promise. Fortunately, New York City itself is beginning to recognize the need to reformulate its response to the issue of homelessness. In a 1993 report, the city described its recent effort to shift its homeless policy from one "aimed at providing basic emergency shelter to a more informed policy that focuses not upon developing shelter after shelter, but upon meeting the service needs of those requesting emergency housing."[28]

Meanwhile, the New York City shelter system continues to fall short. Not only does this mean that the problem of homelessness continues unabated, but it grows worse as the very experience of it creates its own problems and cycles. This is especially true for homeless children. Homelessness threatens their development and interrupts their education even more seriously than poverty alone does. Unless family homelessness is addressed these children will only add to tomorrow's rising statistics of poor and unemployable Americans.

However, the shelter system need not be scrapped entirely. In fact, fundamental elements of the system—such as the transitional housing facility—continue to hold the greatest promise for real solutions. As the following chapters will show, facilities such as HFH's Residential Educational Training centers can serve as effective vehicles for the intensive, comprehensive and sustained assistance essential to real independence. By broadening its outlook to address the *many* problems that cause homelessness—not just a lack of housing, but inadequate education, training, income and family support—the New York City shelter system will finally begin to offer visible results. Such a transformation and restructuring is not only necessary, but also feasible. Only then can we begin to break the tragic cycle of homelessness.

Lydia, Gladys and Christopher
1993

WHEN IS A SHELTER NOT A SHELTER:

The Residential Educational Training Center Model

Homeless policy has faltered most fundamentally because of a well-intentioned but misguided focus on emergency shelter as the primary goal and permanent housing as its immediate follow-up. Ten years ago, this approach may have been enough. A family facing homelessness because of a fire or an illness that has depleted its savings needs little more than that level of assistance; but such a family no longer represents the typical homeless family. Today's family is homeless not because of an individual family emergency, but because of severe *family poverty* and the many problems associated with it.

Today homelessness is less a housing issue than a poverty issue, an education issue, a family support issue and, most importantly, a children's issue. To succeed as anything more than temporary, superficial palliatives, shelters and transitional housing facilities must now address each of these needs. The Homes for the Homeless (HFH) model of Residential Educational Training (RET) centers, developed over the course of seven years of direct service to homeless families, represents the kind of flexible, multifaceted approach now needed. It is comprehensive, family-based, and rooted in the premise that homelessness, and by extension poverty, can end only through education. Equally important, the model has been developed from on-going data collection and program evaluation and has succeeded in helping thousands of New York City's homeless families.

THE RATIONALE

Both field experience and academic research suggest that true success lies in a comprehensive, sustained, family-based program that goes far beyond the issue of housing. The RET center model takes the valuable shelter infrastructure developed in the 1980s and transforms and enriches it, making it less a shelter system than a family education and anti-poverty system.

When Shelter is Not Enough: Problems of Traditional Shelters

More often than not, a homeless family today leaves a shelter for permanent housing little better off than when it entered due to the inadequate provision of crucial services. The problems that caused homelessness are still dangerously intact, with new ones added. Children are frequently worse off, most notably in terms of their education and development. The shelter has served as merely that: a temporary shelter that has briefly provided for the family's most basic physical needs but not its economic or social ones.

The little data available on post-shelter trends illustrate how self-defeating such a system is, and why it must do more to ensure that a family actually accomplishes, on a long-term basis, the successful transition to independent living and permanent housing. New York City's experience offers just one example. According to the New York City Human Resources Administration, *one in every two* homeless families returns to the shelter system after finding housing through the city. Another study found that in 1989, 27 percent of families leaving the city's shelter system returned within seven months. HFH data substantiates such findings: over one-third of the families coming to HFH report that they have been through the city's shelter system at least once before. Nearly half of these families have made three or more trips through the system.[1]

It is impossible to pinpoint for certain what causes such high failure rates. However, HFH believes that the lack of education and support services is key. Today the city of New York requires most family shelters to offer private rooms, supervision, meals and a range of services including assessment, information and referral, health services, child care and housing-placement assistance (see Table 3). Although they have the option to go beyond these minimum services, most shelters in New York City do not. As a result, the majority of homeless families going through the city's shelter system see little more than their basic needs met. They live in spartan, crowded and impersonal surroundings for extended periods, often times waiting over a year for placement in permanent housing. Once there, they are again on their own to face the challenges of raising a family in poverty, with little more than memories of a depressing shelter stay as impetus to avoid repeating the experience.[2]

An Alternative Approach: Developing Family "Learning Centers"

The harsh and frustrating realities of the New York City shelter system formed the basis for the strategy HFH adopted in 1986. More than anything else, HFH's founders were determined to improve the role temporary shelters played in the lives of homeless children and families. The overarching goals: to not only help families meet their immediate needs and ultimately obtain permanent housing, but also to give them the skills and support necessary to succeed long term in establishing their own homes and living independently. Transitional housing facilities offer a way of reaching that goal, providing a unique opportunity for comprehensive, sustained assistance and education.

Table 3: Comparison of Services in NYC – Emergency Shelters vs. RET Center Facilities

	Emergency Shelters	RET Center Facilities
OBJECTIVE	• To provide emergency accommodations until a family finds permanent housing	• To provide educational and social services to address the underlying causes of homelessness
FAMILY SIZE	• 3 members per family	• 3 members per family
FUNDING	• Emergency Assistance • 50% Federal; 25% State; 25% Local	• Emergency Assistance • 50% Federal; 25% State; 25% Local
OPERATING COSTS	• Average cost = $100/day/family • Local share = $25/day/family • Local share = $8.33/day/person	• Average cost = $100/day/family • Local share = $25/day/family • Local share = $8.33/day/person
CASELOAD	• 1 caseworker to 60 families	• 1 caseworker to 20 families
ROOM TYPES	• Single or congregate rooms • Private or congregate bathrooms • Food/Restaurant Allowance	• Furnished private rooms • Private bathrooms • Individual kitchens or congregate dining
SECURITY	• Minimal security	• 24-hour security
DAYCARE	• Not available on-site	• On-site daycare centers
HEALTH CARE	• Not available on-site	• On-site clinics for physicals and preventative medical care • Medical vans provide medical, prenatal and dental care • Referral to community hospitals
DRUG TREATMENT	• Not available on-site	• On-site substance abuse counseling • On-site residential treatment • Referral to community programs
EDUCATION	• Board of Education monitor	• Board of Education monitor • Licensed on-site kindergarten • Afterschool programs on-site • Alternative high school on-site • Parenting and skill-building workshops for adults on-site
RECREATION	• Not available on-site	• On-site recreation, theatre, team sports, and field trips for children • Summer camps for children
HOUSING	• Limited number of housing specialists deployed to hotels	• On-site housing specialists assist families in finding affordable housing • On-site housing workshops help adults build independent living-skills
AFTERCARE	• Not available on-site	• Continued support, follow up and linkages to community programs to help families remain in their housing

HFH is not alone in concluding that such an approach is now necessary. Increasing numbers of scholars and others studying homeless
and poor families argue that economic misfortune and a lack of
housing no longer account for most homelessness; instead, other
social problems do, especially inadequate income, education and
social supports. There is mounting support for the widespread implementation of comprehensive models like the one developed by HFH:
programs that educate and train families, that offer counseling, that
provide diverse forms of family support, from child care to health
care. And because these are, in essence, anti-poverty programs, such
models are applicable nationwide, even in areas where homelessness
is still only probable, and thus still preventable.[3]

Perhaps the most powerful support for the RET center model comes
in the form of a simple comparison. In New York City today, the
average homeless family, after staying in a typical shelter, stands a
one-in-two chance of becoming homeless again. By contrast, roughly
94 percent of the families who have stayed at a RET center remain living
independently in their permanent housing more than a year after
moving out of the center (see Figure 13).[4]

THE COMPONENTS

The Residential Educational Training center represents the core of
the HFH model of transitional housing. In addition to private family-
housing units, RET centers offer comprehensive educational and
training programs. These programs, in turn, are supported by critical, on-site social services such as child care and family counseling (see
Chart 1). Parents are given the opportunity to continue and complete their educations, to acquire independent living skills and to
obtain job training before moving into permanent housing. At the
same time, their children's education, recreation, and health are
assured and any family problems are addressed. RET centers
tap the potential of the transitional shelters; they turn a long

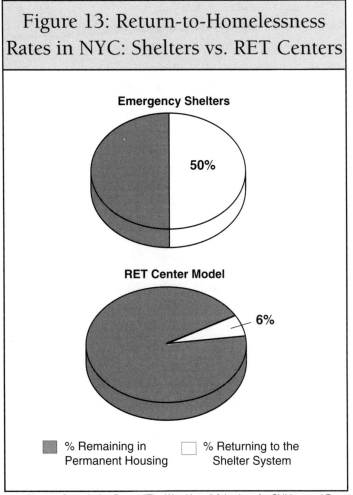

Figure 13: Return-to-Homelessness Rates in NYC: Shelters vs. RET Centers

Emergency Shelters

50%

RET Center Model

6%

▨ % Remaining in   ☐ % Returning to the
   Permanent Housing   Shelter System

Source: Mayor's Commission Report "The Way Home" & Institute for Children and Poverty

Homeless families that lived in traditional emergency shelters have significantly higher return-to-homelessness rates after being placed in permanent housing than those homeless families that received comprehensive services through the Homes for the Homeless RET centers.

Chart 1: The RET Center Model

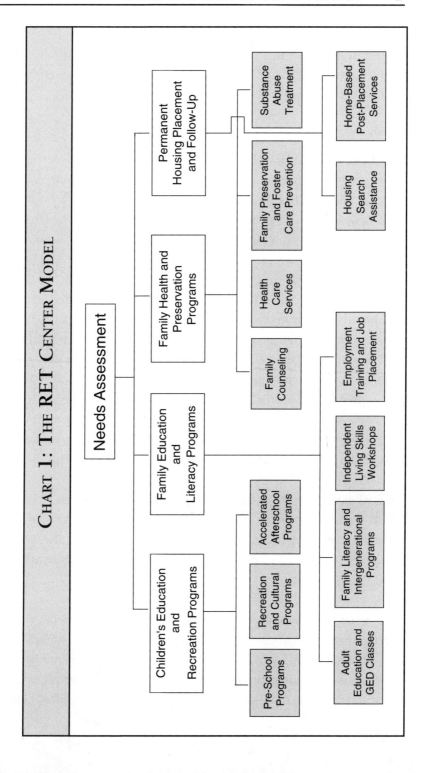

shelter stay into a productive, concentrated period of learning, recovery and preparation, with all the necessary tools and support available on-site.

Putting the Idea to Work: RET Center Operations

HFH has established four RET centers in New York City over the past seven years, and two more are planned. In total, these centers serve roughly 530 families, or 10 percent of New York City's homeless family population. Over the years, HFH has provided services to some 7600 families, including more than 17,300 children.

The oldest center is the Prospect RET center. Located in the South Bronx, where it serves 88 families, the center is a converted hospital purchased in a bankruptcy auction. The Clinton RET center, which accommodates 82 families in Manhattan, was an executive hotel with studios, one-, and two-bedroom suites. HFH bought the building after local real estate trends pushed it into foreclosure. The Staten Island RET center, which serves 117 families, was purchased when a nursing home was shut down. The largest RET center is the Saratoga located in Queens, which serves up to 240 families. This facility, formerly a Holiday Inn Hotel, was also purchased at auction in a bankruptcy sale.

All RET centers have a core staff to ensure their safe and efficient operation. In addition, specialized staff run a combination of education and family support programs. All the centers have a Family Services Department that acts as the clearinghouse and referral mechanism for all family programming.

Each center caters to a specific population of families and offers a variety of programs. Some programs serve all families at the center, such as child care and recreation, while others address specific needs including substance abuse and domestic violence. The primary programs of the HFH model, described in more detail in subsequent chapters, are listed below:

Needs Assessment

When a family first checks in to a RET center, a caseworker in the Family Services Department does a detailed intake profiling the family. Based on this intake, the caseworker develops a service plan, spelling out short- and long-term goals for both parents and children. Through frequent meetings, the caseworkers monitor a family's progress over time. They update the plan at least once every three months.

Children's Education and Recreation Programs

- *Preschool Programs*
  The Jump-Start Program, comprised of a Child Development Center, a Family Literacy Program and an Intergenerational Program, is an innovative, family-based child-care program that provides infants and preschool children with positive stimuli and support to begin their educational and social development.

- *Accelerated Afterschool Programs*
  The Brownstone School, an accelerated afterschool program, aims to compensate for the educational disparities faced by many homeless children. With innovative teaching techniques and a focus on conceptual learning and problem solving, this program instills in children (and their parents) an overall enthusiasm for learning.

- *Recreation Programs*
  Healthy Living Centers provide extracurricular and recreational activities focusing on children's physical and social development, including programs in dance, theater, art and sports. In addition, over 750 homeless children are sent each summer to educational camps operated by Homes for the Homeless. While their two-week stays are filled with swimming, hiking, arts and crafts, and organized play, children also engage in educational activities such as nature talks and conservation projects.

Family Education Programs

- *Adult Education*
  To assist the 60 percent of HFH parents without high school diplomas, each RET center has on-site Alternative High Schools to help adults complete their education and earn their General Equivalency Diplomas (GED). The Alternative High Schools also help students currently in school and recent dropouts.

- *Independent Living Skills Workshops*
  The PLUS (Practical Living/Useful Skills) program offers a series of six-week workshops to help prepare families for independent living. Topics include parenting, domestic violence, child development, housing maintenance, budgeting, health and nutrition, AIDS and sexually transmitted diseases, and self-esteem. As an extension of PLUS, caseworker and peer-led support groups also offer more informal arenas for discussion of these issues.

- *Employment Training*
  Train and Gain (TAG), an innovative employment training and apprenticeship program, offers on-the-job training in a variety of entry-level positions. In addition, topical workshops prepare program participants for the job search and for the challenges and responsibilities of full-time employment.

Family Health and Preservation Programs

- *Family Counseling*
  With a caseload of 20 families each, caseworkers facilitate and reinforce the individual goals laid out in a family's service plan and help the family deal with unexpected problems or crises. Families meet with their caseworkers at least once a week.

- *Health Services*
  In collaboration with other community health-care providers, HFH provides on-site preventive services as well as prenatal and pediatric care, dental care and immunizations for children.

- *Family Preservation/Foster Care Prevention*
  Families experiencing stress or violence have access to HFH's Family Crisis Nurseries. The nurseries provide a temporary safe haven for children at risk of child abuse and neglect, along with immediate access to support services for their parents. A longer-term residential program, Together in Emotional Strength (TIES), is available for those families struggling with alcohol or drug abuse and who are also at risk of child abuse or neglect. The Family Reunification and Preservation Program works to stabilize parents who are in danger of losing their children to out-of-home placement and to reunify families whose children are already in foster care.

- *Substance Abuse Treatment*
  On-site substance abuse counseling is offered through innovative family-based programs developed in conjunction with outside treatment programs. These supportive programs include children as part of the therapeutic process.

Permanent Housing Assistance

- *Housing Search Assistance*
  Housing specialists assist all families in their search for permanent housing. These specialists link families with sources of public and private housing, including apartments with private landlords.

- *Home-Based Services*
  The PLUS INC (PLUS In New Communities) program was developed to ensure a smooth transition to permanent housing. Working with a caseload of roughly 40 families, each PLUS INC caseworker maintains contact with families up to one year after they leave the RET center. They encourage families to continue working on their service plan goals, link them to community-based agencies, and connect them to school-based programs in their new neighborhoods.

HFH has developed these programs based on a combination of direct service experience and on-going data collection and evaluation. Before wider application to all RET centers, a program undergoes a period of pilot operation at one center where it is closely monitored and modified when necessary. Programs showing poor results are discontinued altogether; those that prove effective are expanded to other centers.

A key component of program development and evaluation is the HFH data collection system. All four RET centers are linked to a central information network that is continually updated and accessible to all HFH staff. In addition to program assessment and evaluation, the system tracks demographic trends and individual family progress and problems.

With such extensive data and over seven years of direct service, HFH has successfully begun to combat family homelessness, helping a full 94 percent of participating families regain and retain permanent housing. Furthermore, HFH believes this model can be replicated with equal or better success elsewhere, and not only in the fight against homelessness, but in the fight against poverty.

Joan and Kadeem
1993

BREAKING
THE
CYCLE:

Educating the Children

Of the many barriers impeding homeless families, inadequate education is among the most devastating. The reality is as simple as it is stark: without education there is little hope. Today education is the fundamental tool with which Americans build and mend their lives; without it, poverty cannot be overcome. Poverty can be alleviated temporarily and its worst symptoms treated, but it will remain firmly and relentlessly entrenched, besieging generation after generation of families. To truly *stop* such a cycle requires sustained, quality education.

Educating our nation's growing numbers of poor children is the most basic and promising step we can take toward breaking this cycle. Homeless children need education most desperately of all. They are even *more* undereducated and at risk of severe, generational poverty than are other poor children. The very experience of homelessness further diminishes their already meager chances for healthy development and academic success.

Tragically, current policy largely fails these children. With a narrow focus on emergency shelter and housing still prevailing, the fundamental link between homelessness and undereducation continues to be ignored. By contrast, the RET center model of transitional housing places education at its core. Homes for the Homeless strives to educate homeless children and their families as a means of true, generational *transition*—from homelessness and poverty to permanent self-sufficiency.

THE RATIONALE

Although the U.S. Department of Education estimated that even in the mid-1980s, 30 percent of homeless children did not attend school at all, other experts believe that figure to be more than 50 percent. Even when they do attend school, such children tend to be absent more often and to drop out at a higher rate than non-homeless children. They are also likely to receive poor grades and are often put in special education classrooms or held back a grade (see Table 4).[1]

New York City statistics offer a startling illustration of these trends. One study of New York City homeless children in the public school system found that homelessness severely harmed students' academic progress. Homeless children only erratically attended school, repeatedly transferred schools, and most tested below grade level in both reading and math. Another New York City study revealed that only half of the students with special education needs continued to receive those services once they became homeless.[2]

More recent data collected by HFH reveals just how common, and how much worse, such educational gaps are today. In a 1992 study, HFH found that in comparison to New York City's non-homeless children of similar ages, the homeless children coming through its RET centers were:

- 8 times more likely to repeat a grade
- 4 times more likely to drop out of school
- 3 times more likely to be placed in a special education program, and
- 2 times more likely to score lower on standardized tests (see Figure 14).[3]

TABLE 4: DEMOGRAPHIC PROFILE OF HOMELESS SCHOOL-AGED CHILDREN

Characteristic	1992
Gender	
Female	37%
Male	63%
Average Age	9
Average Grade Level	4th
Elementary	65%
Jr. High & High School	35%
Educational Status	
Perform Below Reading Grade Level	62%
Perform Below Math Grade Level	78%
Placed in Special Education	24%
Repeated a Grade	37%
Source: Institute for Children and Poverty	

More than one-third of homeless school-aged children in NYC have repeated a grade; one out of four have been placed in special education classes; and the overwhelming majority perform below grade level in reading and math.

Brownstone School
1993

"Homeless children feel that everything is either done to them, or done for them. The Brownstone School philosophy of learning gives them a chance to gain a greater sense of control over their education and lives."

— Brownstone School Director

In the 1992 school year, nearly half of all school-age children entering HFH's facilities had attended at least two different schools. Another third had attended three separate schools, while 13 percent had been to at least four. Extended absenteeism was also common. Before they came to HFH, the same group of children had missed, on average, three weeks of school. Worse yet, 20 percent of these children had missed at least *six* weeks of classes, or one-sixth of the school year.[4]

Developmental problems often strike children whose families become homeless. Numerous studies have documented significant cognitive as well as physical developmental delays among homeless infants and children, especially in the areas of motor, language and interpersonal skills. Many preschoolers display severe, multiple developmental lags and even signs of regression. And while it is critically important to detect and treat such delays in children, parents overwhelmed by poverty and homelessness often cannot identify these problems, much less get help for them.[5]

Unstable Learning: The Effect of Homelessness on Education

Homeless children suffer educational and developmental problems for a variety of reasons. Chief among them is the instability that fractures so many aspects of a homeless family's life. Uprooted from their homes and neighborhoods and separated from friends, homeless children lack the environmental stability and consistency critical to healthy development and effective education. Instead, they face a world that is uncertain, stressful, and often dangerous. Moreover, as families move between temporary homes, homeless children miss classes and change schools repeatedly, sometimes becoming "lost" to the school system, no longer tracked by school officials or teachers.[6]

Not surprisingly, this basic struggle to survive also interferes with parents' ability to perform their role in children's growth. Preoccupied or overwhelmed, homeless parents are often unable to provide

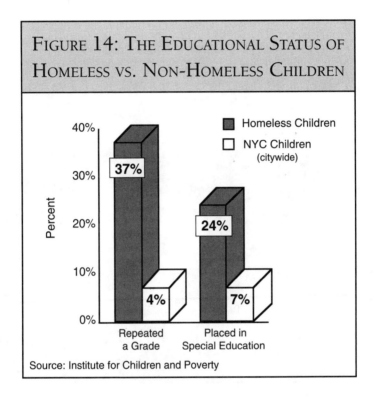

FIGURE 14: THE EDUCATIONAL STATUS OF HOMELESS VS. NON-HOMELESS CHILDREN

Source: Institute for Children and Poverty

Being homeless can have a devastating effect on a child's educational achievement – over one third have repeated a grade and one quarter have been placed into a special education class.

Saratoga RET Center

1992

"For most of these kids, poverty and homelessness has impeded their development in nearly every area — physically, psychologically and academically. With our Jump-Start Program we see changes in a matter of six weeks. You can't imagine what a pleasure it is to see this happen."

— Director, Saratoga RET center's
Child Development Center

fully for their children's developmental and educational needs. Infants and young children frequently receive inadequate stimulation and attention from parents too harried, lonely or depressed to attend to them, while older children receive very little academic encouragement or assistance. And with the population of homeless families becoming younger, more and more parents are simply too inexperienced to know that they should provide these things, let alone figure out how. Financial limitations hobble families still further; toys, books and other developmental stimulants often remain unaffordable luxuries when there is so little money for rent or food.[7]

Forces outside the family are also to blame. Shelters, with their physical constraints and limited privacy, severely restrict children, who are often unable to explore the environment beyond their family's assigned space. Children often become confused and intimidated by the strangers and chaos that constantly surround them. Moreover, shelters frequently maintain only limited coordination with local schools, further hampering a child's ability to sustain his or her education. Even in the highly developed New York City temporary-housing system, only a small fraction of facilities offer any kind of educational support services for homeless children (see Figure 15).[8]

The school system itself hurts homeless children. In 1989, the U.S. Department of Education estimated that over a quarter of school-age homeless children were being denied access to education. The barriers are many: the children face an obstacle course of residency, guardianship and immunization requirements; record keeping systems are often ineffective; and transportation is frequently lacking. Teachers, meanwhile, often know little, if anything, about homeless students' circumstances or how homelessness affects children's education. As a result, such children's academic needs may go unrecognized, untreated or misunderstood.[9]

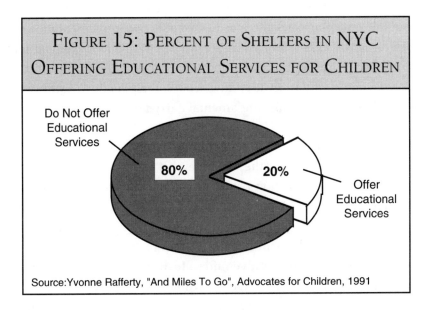

FIGURE 15: PERCENT OF SHELTERS IN NYC OFFERING EDUCATIONAL SERVICES FOR CHILDREN

Do Not Offer Educational Services

80%

20%

Offer Educational Services

Source:Yvonne Rafferty, "And Miles To Go", Advocates for Children, 1991

Education is the key to helping homeless families achieve economic and social independence and must be the basic component of every service plan.

Most emergency shelters and schools neglect to address and sometimes even exacerbate these problems, reflecting a wider policy failure. Although both federal and local regulations provide for the education of homeless children, such laws are generally too narrow, too vague or simply not enforced. For example, the federal McKinney Act guarantees homeless children's access to school, yet many of the resulting state plans lack the specifics for effective implementation or enforcement. Texas offers just one example. While its state plan for homeless children's education recognizes that inadequate transportation prevents many from attending school, the plan does nothing to establish a *solution* to this fundamental barrier.[10]

The federal government itself has failed more generally. Within months of the enactment of the McKinney Act, the agency charged with implementing its education provisions was sued. Not only was the federal Department of Education failing to distribute federal funds to states, it was not adequately monitoring or providing guidelines for them. Indeed, as late as mid-1990, it had not monitored *any* states receiving McKinney money. Even after a 1990 revision of the McKinney Act expanded the reach and state coordination of its education provisions, the program remained riddled with administrative problems, noncompliance, confusion and chronic underfunding at all levels.[11]

Creating a New Cycle: Homes For the Homeless Education Programs

Determined to avoid the mistakes and shortcomings of previous policies, HFH puts children's education at the very forefront of its strategy. Its guiding philosophy is twofold: proper education is necessary both in the short-term, to mitigate the potentially damaging effects of homelessness on children, and in the long-run, to finally end the cycle of poverty in this generation. Equally important, HFH recognizes that homeless children are not only extraordinarily vulnerable, but also resilient and adaptive, ready to succeed as well as any other child, given sufficient support.

Our programs build on the abundant research demonstrating the positive and long-lasting effects—on the entire family—of early childhood intervention. Numerous studies have concluded that the best time to help poor and disadvantaged families is when their children are very young. It is during these early years that children are at the same time most susceptible to harm and most receptive to positive influences. Their young parents also tend to be more highly motivated at this stage.[12]

HFH also bases its children's programs on the increasing evidence (including data collected from our own work in the field) that children from disadvantaged backgrounds do best in accelerated, rather than remedial, education programs. We also recognize that for homeless children in particular, recreational and artistic opportunities are critical, both for their physical and intellectual development and as an outlet for the emotions and frustrations that often accompany life in poverty. The children's programs at the HFH RET centers work together to provide what growing numbers of researchers recommend but too few policy makers include in their plans: continuous, stable, quality education that is family-based and tailored to the individual needs of homeless children.[13]

THE COMPONENTS

Each RET center offers a continuum of educational services for children, from infant development to adolescent dropout prevention. An educational plan developed by family caseworkers for each family upon arrival at a center guides children's participation in the programs. Caseworkers then make sure that the plan is coordinated with other services the family is receiving. In addition, they serve as liaisons, working closely with public school teachers in both in-house and outside programs. This relationship ensures continuity and prevents the too-common situation where teachers fail to adequately reach homeless children or understand the educational challenges they face.

A Jump-Start on the Future: Early Childhood Education Programs

Despite the substantial evidence that early education encourages cognitive and social development in children while also producing long-term educational benefits, many children in the United States are not enrolled in preschool. This is particularly true of low-income and homeless children. In a 1992 survey of families residing at HFH RET centers, we found that nearly 80 percent of school-age children had not attended any school prior to kindergarten. In contrast, 60 percent of children from upper socioeconomic groups and 45 percent from middle socioeconomic groups had benefited from at least one year of preschool (see Figure 16).[14]

Not surprisingly, this discrepancy is primarily a function of a family's ability to pay for such programs. While Head Start (a federally financed preschool program) was designed to ensure that low-income children could attend preschool, it serves less than 20 percent of all eligible children. Furthermore, the great majority of existing Head Start programs are part-day, part-year programs only. Homeless children are especially likely to miss out, because local program directors often prefer to maintain continuity in their programs, a goal that precludes placement of children living only temporarily in emergency shelters and facing an uncertain future.[15]

To remedy these conditions, HFH developed the Jump-Start program. Unlike traditional day care, which generally resembles a kind of supervised baby-sitting service that lacks an educational component, the Jump-Start program focuses on the physical, social and cognitive development of children and the support of their families. Today, serving more than 250 children under the age of six living in the RET centers, Jump-Start is comprised of a Child Development Center, a family literacy program, and an intergenerational program at all four of HFH's RET centers.

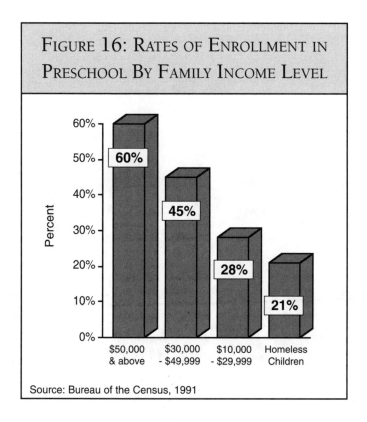

FIGURE 16: RATES OF ENROLLMENT IN PRESCHOOL BY FAMILY INCOME LEVEL

Source: Bureau of the Census, 1991

Although participation in preschool leads to lower drop out rates, and lower rates of teenage pregnancy, criminal behavior and welfare dependency, homeless children participate in these programs significantly less than children of other socioeconomic groups.

Jump-Start Program

1993

Charlene, 21, attributes her two-year-old son's rapid progress to Jump-Start's unique philosophy: "At first I thought they'd just be baby-sitters. Then they invited us to watch the children and I saw how much they were teaching them. They cater to the children, but only to a point. The teachers really encourage them to be independent."

"When we arrived, Curtis didn't know how to interact with other children. He was really aggressive. Now he plays with his friends and even calls their names when he sees them in the hallways. And he knows how to share; he offers the other children toys when they come to our room. He's changed a lot in only three months, and most of that I owe to child care."

The Child Development Centers (CDC) form the centerpiece of the Jump-Start program and serve both infants and preschool-age children. The infant care component offers children a nurturing environment where they receive critical and engaging stimuli for their mental and social development. Infant rooms are designed to provide the youngest infants stimuli in the areas of sight and sound, and to give older infants more advanced psychomotor activities. Preschool children are offered a different kind of Jump-Start on their education. For them, the CDC employs a variation of the High/Scope curriculum, an educational method known for its effectiveness with at-risk or disadvantaged children. Developed at the University of Michigan, the High/Scope model is child-directed. By using a child's own interests to plan his or her day with the guidance of supportive adults, the activities not only accomplish an immediate goal (such as painting, participating in mock Olympics, or planting vegetables), but also foster a sense of control and initiative in the child. As both researchers and HFH have found, such activities enrich both educational and social development of children: they incorporate motor skills activities, communication and teamwork, creativity, logic, and an understanding of spatial relationships.[16]

CDC activities also involve parents. HFH has found that many homeless parents lack a support network from which to get accurate information or to voice their own pride, fears or reflections about their child's development (see also Chapter 4). Therefore, Jump-Start programs strive to engage and support parents. Teachers arrange weekly conferences with parents to discuss their child's needs and progress. Parents themselves participate in the infant activities, thereby gaining a wider knowledge of their child's development process, from infancy through the toddler stages. Parents are closely involved in the preschool program as well. They are encouraged to view the CDC not simply as a drop-off service, but as a place where their child will truly learn and develop through a variety of engaging activities, including those that parents can lead in their own homes.

The family literacy and intergenerational components of Jump-Start complement the Child Development Centers. Together In Learning is a family literacy program that develops the literacy skills of parents— through activities such as group readings and library trips—while promoting learning as a shared family value. The intergenerational program works in conjunction with local senior citizen centers to sponsor workshops on puppetry, clay-molding, and paper maché. These activities allow children to interact with older adults, who provide them with an abundance of attention and care. In addition, their parents reap the benefits of senior role models who can share their own experiences of parenting children.

The Learning Fast-track: Accelerated Education Programs

One of HFH's most successful programs serves homeless children ages 5 through 13 living at its RET centers. Located adjacent to the Prospect RET center, the Brownstone School (which takes its name from its location in a renovated historic Brownstone building) compensates for the disparity in educational opportunities available to homeless children by supplementing their public school education. Conducted after regular school hours, this accelerated after-school program is based on the premise that children who are behind should not be placed in a "slow lane" or a remedial program to catch up, but rather into the "fast lane," or into a program similar to those designed for "gifted and talented" children.

Guided by the educational model developed by Henry Levin at Stanford University, the Brownstone School emphasizes a low student-to-teacher ratio with a high degree of individualization for each student's needs. The model stresses the teaching of concepts, analysis and problem-solving, instead of the more traditional repetition and drills. It also instills and strengthens the fundamental educational building blocks of reading, writing, science and mathematics. Enhancing these innovative teaching techniques and educational

Brownstone School

1993

At 11, Jose had witnessed his father abusing his mother more times than he could remember. After one too many times, he tried to defend himself and his mother—by attempting to shoot his father. After that incident, Jose and his mother left his father, and, with nowhere to turn, arrived at the Prospect RET center. Prior to enrolling at the Brownstone School, Jose was delinquent at school and was placed in special education classes. Brownstone teachers worked with him to find his interests, and, more importantly, his strengths, which turned out to be computers and math. Jose is now the resident "computer genius" at Brownstone; he is so far ahead that he acts as a teaching assistant for the younger children.

programs are interactive learning tools and field work, such as the LEGO-logo computer program for math building, a community garden for science experiments, and journal writing for language-arts and reading.[17]

These features, coupled with strong student-teacher relationships, allow children at the Brownstone School to develop enhanced learning ability, greater self-confidence, and a sense of accomplishment. High expectations, deadlines for clearly identified performance levels and stimulating instructional materials are also key in this process. Above all, the Brownstone staff strives to provide a challenging, stable environment that encourages homeless children through new and non-threatening educational activities.

Like Jump-Start, the Brownstone School sponsors activities to encourage parents to become directly involved in their children's education. Parents work with teachers and children to develop and complete "learning contracts" based on subject areas chosen by the children. Family-literacy workshops are also offered, as well as group field trips and family projects, such as working in the community garden and mother-teen workshops. The staff also facilitates greater collaboration between the parents and the public schools by urging parents to use their children's teacher as a source of advice and by encouraging parent-teacher conferences. Brownstone teachers often accompany parents to these conferences and explore a child's new school with parents when the family moves into permanent housing.

Kids Just Want to Have Fun: Recreation and Cultural Programs at the Healthy Living Centers

Extracurricular activities are essential to round out a child's educational and social development. Social, physical and artistic activities are especially important for homeless children, who are often consumed by the anxiety and confusion they feel concerning their families. They miss their old neighborhoods and friends and often feel unwelcome or uncomfortable in a new school, where they are sometimes taunted and stigmatized for being homeless. Space limitations frequently hamper homeless children and adolescents as well, depriving them of the exercise and exploration so important to healthy development.

To alleviate such stresses and provide enjoyable, supportive activities for children residing at RET centers, HFH created the Healthy Living Centers. These recreation centers serve as hubs for a variety of activities. They furnish critical opportunities for self-expression, social acceptance, accomplishment, and physical exercise for school-age children. The Healthy Living Centers also sponsor preventative programs and offer alternatives to the destructive or violent behavior to which so many of today's poor children fall victim. The only requirement for participation in the recreation center's daily activities is attendance at school.

Theater, art, dance and poetry allow children to build a sense of accomplishment and to express feelings they might not otherwise articulate, from typical adolescent frustrations to those about poverty and homelessness. Participation in sports teams, theater companies, and local Boy and Girl Scout troops encourage cooperation and teach socialization skills. Workshops and rap sessions on substance abuse, AIDS, pregnancy and crime help children develop coping and decision-making skills. In addition, the Healthy Living Centers sponsor special outings to popular Madison Square Garden or Shea Stadium sports events, as well as to Broadway theater productions.

Many activities at the Healthy Living Centers complement education. The staff offers intensive homework assistance and organizes regular trips to local libraries. In addition, children and teens produce monthly newsletters at the centers, reporting on RET center news and events

Saratoga Healthy Living Center

1993

For many children, boys in particular, the male staff members at recreation are the first positive role models they've had. "We don't give them pity," says the Director of the Saratoga Healthy Living Center. "We talk about what it feels like to be homeless, and tell them that they have to realize their family is going through a rough time, but that it's temporary, and they won't be here forever. That's exactly what we suggest they say to the kids who sometimes make fun of them. 'You're going to survive this and be stronger from it,' I say. Through our encouragement and focus on their strengths and abilities they begin to see themselves what they can achieve."

and publishing their artwork and poetry. These publications are part of an overall effort to build community and group support among the children and families staying at HFH. Collaborations with neighborhood organizations and volunteers serve similar goals. Such projects, including a program in which non-homeless teens from surrounding areas participate in RET center activities, provide important links with the community, where homeless families often feel unwanted or isolated.

The Healthy Living Centers also strive to bolster homeless children's self-esteem and sense of identity through activities that explore and celebrate the diverse cultures that make up both the immediate environment and the surrounding neighborhood. Art and dance programs offered in collaboration with various New York City cultural organizations, such as El Grupo Morivivi (also known as the East Harlem School of Music) and the Department of Cultural Affairs expose children to a rich assortment of cultural experiences and activities. We take a multicultural approach: holiday projects, for instance, celebrate Our Lady of Guadalupe, Bodhi Day, Hanukkah, Kwanzaa and Haiti Independence Day, in addition to Christmas. Furthermore, the staff and volunteers of the centers themselves reflect the multi-ethnic, diverse population of New York City and serve as role models for the children. All of these programs reinforce children's sense of community and helps them begin to feel a part of their new neighborhoods.

Two annual summer camps in upstate New York near Bear Mountain extend opportunities for recreational education and therapy even further. Camps Lanowa and Kiwago invite children on a two-week escape from urban life. More than 750 homeless children from welfare hotels, city shelters, and RET centers come to camp, often swimming, boating, fishing and camping for the first time. Cultural and artistic activities are also central: campers dance and perform at the camp theater, create artwork and organize "International Days" devoted to learning about foreign customs, costumes, food and songs. Older participants go on overnight hiking trips and learn survival and teamwork skills. And as in the Healthy Living Centers, education figures prominently, but pleasurably throughout.

Finally, like all RET center children's programming, the Healthy Living Centers involve parents. Both individually and in groups, parents meet with staff to discuss children's attendance at school, contact with teachers, ties with the local schools and other matters of concern. The staff works to develop trust so that when they notice that children are experiencing problems, they can work supportively with parents to address them.

THE RESULTS: IT CAN CHANGE

After years of operating, evaluating and fine-tuning these programs, we have seen encouraging results. Homeless children, whom statistics predict would otherwise accrue alarming developmental lags and educational problems, avoid those pitfalls during their participation in RET center programs. In fact, these children flourish. Data gathered from HFH's child education and recreation components reveals that children in these programs achieve significant gains, not only academically, but also socially and emotionally.

The Jump-Start program has shown some of the most promising results. Overall, we have found that our Child Development Centers have an enormous impact on children, especially when compared to conventional child-care methods (see Figure 17). Children show rapid developmental, social and emotional growth in as little as eight weeks. Their language skills improve dramatically and their attention spans lengthen. They exhibit more cooperative behavior. Their self-confidence grows and they become more spirited and alert. In addition, children experience growth spurts and weight gain.[18]

Jump-Start Child Development Center

1993

Lisa, age twenty-four, credits the Child Development Center with helping her four year-old son Reginald overcome the developmental set-backs he suffered during her drug addiction. "When I was doing drugs, I dragged him through my addiction. Reggie never had a chance to be around kids, but now he's in a setting with other children, and he's learning to socialize. Each week he moves closer and closer to his age group. He's growing up the way he's supposed to grow up, instead of the way I was bringing him up."

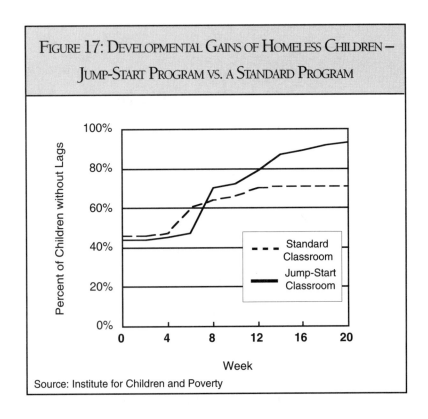

FIGURE 17: DEVELOPMENTAL GAINS OF HOMELESS CHILDREN —
JUMP-START PROGRAM VS. A STANDARD PROGRAM

Source: Institute for Children and Poverty

Homeless preschoolers manifest a number of developmental lags, as revealed by standardized tests. However, in just weeks the children in the RET Child Development Centers show marked improvements in the areas of gross and fine motor, language comprehension and social skills. Children participating in the Jump-Start program exhibit even greater gains than those children participating in standard day care.

Brownstone School students also make extraordinary academic gains. After six months of attending the Brownstone School, the children's scoring potential in reading had risen by half, from less than 40 percent to 60 percent. Their scoring potential in math, meanwhile, more than doubled, from 23 percent to roughly 50 percent (see Figure 18). In addition, many Brownstone students won academic awards from their public schools in reading, science, spelling and math.[19]

The Brownstone School has also had a positive impact on school attendance. At 92 percent, the public school attendance rate among Brownstone School students is almost 30 percent higher than the citywide attendance rate for homeless children (63 percent) (see Figure 19). School attendance is also higher for Brownstone School students when compared to the system-wide average of 86 percent for all children in New York City. And while 60 percent of the absences attributed to HFH students *not* attending the Brownstone School were unexcused, only 35 percent of the absences of the Brownstone students were unexcused or unrelated to illness.[20]

Finally, the Brownstone School also appears to enhance parental involvement in children's education. Where roughly 26 percent of HFH parents whose children do not attend Brownstone frequently visit their children's school, an astounding *86 percent* of Brownstone parents visit the school and their child's teacher often. Moreover, when parents at the RET center housing the Brownstone School were asked to name the person they would consult about their child's education, nearly all identified Brownstone teachers. As research has shown, such partnerships are likely to motivate parents to continue communicating with their children's teachers in later years, as well as to be more generally involved in their children's education.[21]

Brownstone School
1993

Michelle, 12, began attending the Brownstone School when she, her mother, and her four brothers and sisters moved to the Prospect RET center shortly after her father died of AIDS. Even though the family has moved on to permanent housing, Michelle still comes to the after-school program three times a week. "You learn more at Brownstone than in school," she says. "I used to be in the lowest level reading class, now I'm in the highest." Since attending the Brownstone School, Michelle has received numerous awards at her public school: a trip to Washington, DC for high achievement, two certificates of outstanding achievement, a history award for the highest average, a medal for math excellence, and her public school's Group Leader Award. She is applying for admission to the prestigious Hostos-Lincoln Academy of Science for high school.

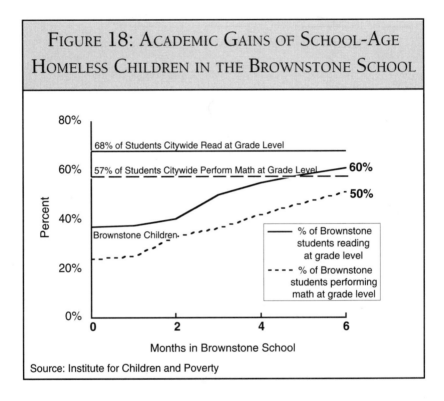

FIGURE 18: ACADEMIC GAINS OF SCHOOL-AGE HOMELESS CHILDREN IN THE BROWNSTONE SCHOOL

Source: Institute for Children and Poverty

When homeless children learn in an accelerated environment they show remarkable gains in as little as six months. Children increase their scores in math and reading comprehension nearly two-fold.

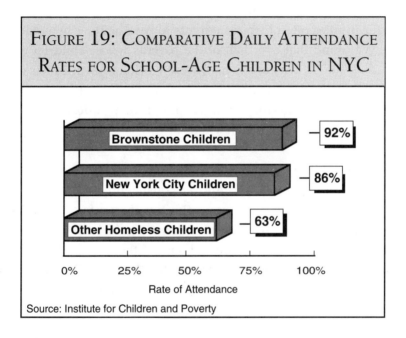

FIGURE 19: COMPARATIVE DAILY ATTENDANCE
RATES FOR SCHOOL-AGE CHILDREN IN NYC

Brownstone Children — 92%

New York City Children — 86%

Other Homeless Children — 63%

0%   25%   50%   75%   100%

Rate of Attendance

Source: Institute for Children and Poverty

Studies have shown that high rates of absenteeism, particularly among low-income students, predicts subsequent dropping out. As a result HFH closely monitors the school attendance of all its school-age children. Children who participated in the Brownstone School had higher rates of school attendance when compared to other homeless children and New York City students system-wide.

Parents also get involved more directly by frequently volunteering for the programs in which their children participate, whether at the Brownstone School or in other HFH programs. Even more importantly, watching and helping their children flourish in educational activities often inspires parents to resume their own education. We found that over half of the parents whose children were attending the Brownstone School were working toward their own GED (General Equivalency Degree). Overwhelmingly, the reason given by these parents for wanting to pursue their education was "to set a good example for my children."[22]

The Healthy Living Centers also help homeless children. We have found that staff, parents and children consistently praise the recreation centers and the many opportunities they offer. Parents are pleased that their children have a healthy outlet for both their energy and the stress of living without a home of their own. Meanwhile, children enthusiastically embrace the Health Living Centers, often participating in activities for nearly the entire time the centers are open each day.

The staff has also observed the positive effects of recreational activities. Over time they have seen children achieve great strides intellectually and emotionally. Recreation helps many children adjust to their new neighborhoods and helps them develop an interest in extracurricular activities. Perhaps most importantly, they begin to improve at school, not only academically, but also socially.

For homeless children, who spend roughly nine to 12 months of their lives without a permanent home, HFH programs like the Jump-Start CDC's, the Brownstone School and the Healthy Living Centers provide vital educational opportunities and creative outlets too frequently absent from their young lives. Such programs also give these children the opportunity to develop relationships and to nurture their capacity for initiative, curiosity and independence.

The important link of parental involvement is also established and strengthened. Above all, the programs work to initiate a broad learning momentum that ensures *future* educational achievement for these children.

Laura and Jasmine
1993

SUPPORTING CHILDREN BY SUPPORTING PARENTS:

Adult and Family Education

For many homeless families, education is badly needed, not only for the children, but also for their parents. Homeless families are typically headed by young parents who lack even a high school diploma. This, coupled with virtually no work experience, gives them little chance of obtaining jobs to support their families. Their educational needs extend to more practical areas. New to parenting and to living independently, they often lack basic skills in areas ranging from child nutrition and discipline to managing family finances. Not comfortable in an educational environment, they often avoid participating in their children's learning, to the detriment of all involved.

As basic as these needs are, few government or emergency shelter programs address them. While many facilities refer homeless families to job training, such programs are often inappropriate for or inaccessible to homeless parents. Other education and training programs are simply too limited, reaching few of those in need.

Too many view the issue of education too narrowly, ignoring the often critical need for instruction in the area of day-to-day skill development.

However, as intergenerational poverty, undereducation, and the homeless situation have gotten worse across the country, more comprehensive programs have begun to emerge as the only realistic approach for families with so few resources. Such programs, including those offered at HFH's RET centers, are family-based and recognize the numerous, interrelated hurdles that must be overcome by homeless families. Although gainful employment and self-sufficiency are the ultimate goals, the programs begin with family support and education. Equally important, they are flexible; family participation is based on individual needs, circumstances and preferences. For the first time, many homeless families are finding the resources and support they need to build a future.

THE RATIONALE

Increasing numbers of homeless parents, like their children, are severely undereducated. Although the homeless population continues to be a very diverse one, a growing majority of homeless heads-of-household lack the basic qualifications necessary for a job that provides for a family. Today, most homeless parents have a high school education or less and little, if any, employment experience.[1]

Such trends are particularly disturbing given the pivotal role education plays in moving people out of poverty. As numerous studies have demonstrated, economic opportunity and mobility are generally tied directly to educational achievment. In today's job market, where information and service industries predominate, this is truer than ever. Jobs that require few skills or little training are not only decreasing in number but in wage level; the manufacturing and other positions that supported a family of four 20 years ago are simply disappearing.

Furthermore, employers today tend to require higher levels of education and experience, even in relatively low-skill jobs.[2]

Today, the typical job available to a woman with a high school education and minimal work experience would pay only about $5 to $6 per hour ($10,000-12,000 per year, based on 40-hour work weeks, 50 weeks a year) and offer little opportunity for advancement. Yet for most poor and homeless women, that same job would have to support an entire family. It would also have to cover full-time child care, an expenditure that consumes one-quarter of poor families' income, on average. That's when it's available at all. Health care costs would also take a hefty chunk of that salary, since most jobs of this type do not provide family health insurance. Finally, there are housing costs. As housing advocates have made clear, a poor family today confronts a tremendous challenge in obtaining and retaining housing of any kind, much less a decent, safe home conducive to raising healthy children. And the future housing situation looks bleaker still.[3]

A lack of education resonates even beyond these crucial issues of income. Children suffer on several levels. In addition to their obvious economic deprivation, they risk undereducation themselves. The link between parents' educational achievement and their children's has been firmly established. Just as children whose parents had a limited education tend to become undereducated, so do children of well-educated parents seem to go farther academically. Key, of course, is the general lack of educational opportunity available to low-income Americans. Also relevant to this cycle of undereducation is the tendency of lower-educated parents not to get involved in their children's educational activities, in part because they may not realize the importance of such activities or feel comfortable participating in them.[4]

HFH has found this to be true in many cases. Often because they feel ill-equipped in academic matters, or because they were discouraged

Alternative High School

1993

"We find that reading and math levels for homeless parents are even lower than reported—if a mother dropped out of high school in the 10th grade, we find her actual comprehension level is 4th or 5th grade. These kids were left behind way before they left school."

— Clinton RET Center
Alternative High School Teacher

themselves in school, homeless parents keep their distance from their children's education, rarely reading to them or assisting with school assignments. Sometimes they are intimidated by their children's teachers and so may not get involved in school matters or activities. For similar reasons, such parents tend not to encourage their children academically or to hold high expectations, even if they retain hope that the children will succeed. Some teachers often misinterpret such attitudes or assume that uninvolved parents do not care about their children's education.[5]

Despite the obvious need for parent education and job training, it is generally ignored as a subject of homeless policy. While some federal initiatives have begun to allocate funds for adult literacy, basic education and job training, these programs are quite limited and garner only a tiny fraction of federal homeless money (see Chapter 1). Scattered state and local programs also exist, but like their federal counterparts, they reach only certain populations and often only provide assistance for short periods of time. For the most part, this essential area is simply disregarded, even in locales that otherwise adopt a relatively comprehensive approach to homelessness. In New York City, for example, family shelters are required to offer private rooms, access to three nutritional meals, and supervision. In addition, a range of services must be provided, including assessment, recreation, information and referral, health services, child care and housing placement services, but not programs in adult literacy, education or job training.[6]

Giving Homeless Families a Chance: Addressing Parental Education Needs

Our RET center model recognizes that education must play a central role in the lives of homeless families. Furthermore, we build on education's potential as a vehicle for true, lasting change for entire families. Without question, parents are key. Embracing innovative, family-based education techniques, HFH programs work with both parents and children, alone and together, as students and as teachers. In the process, families build practical skills, increase their chances in the job market and strengthen their relationships with each other. The overriding goal is to provide education to every member of the family and to encourage education as a lifelong pursuit.

Numerous studies have documented the positive, far-reaching effects—on both parents and children—of programs that provide education and support to parents. Not only does parental behavior and parent-child interaction improve, but parents' own personal development is enhanced, including a greater sense of self-control, improved coping skills and higher self-esteem. In the process, the family develops a greater chance of becoming economically self-sufficient. As poverty researchers have pointed out, families with intensive needs (like many homeless families) require programs that do more than focus solely on children. Parents, and the family as a whole, need support and assistance.[7]

Most importantly, research suggests that such programs produce positive "two-generation" effects, a benefit of particular importance in the struggle to break the cycle of poverty. Those programs with the greatest promise are comprehensive, continuous and intensive. This is one of the reasons we believe transitional, supported housing holds so much promise. By offering the opportunity for sustained comprehensive work with families for extended periods of time, transitional housing programs like those provided in RET centers satisfy the most crucial requirements for intergenerational success.[8]

THE COMPONENTS

The parental and family programs at HFH's RET centers complement and reinforce programs tailored for children. While children attend classes, parents attend classes. As children participate in activities at the Healthy Living Centers or the Child Development Centers, parents prepare for full-time employment and permanent housing. At other times, parents and children learn together. Whatever the program, the goal is a strengthened, better-educated family, fortified not only to return to the community, but to flourish there in work, school and family life.

Acquiring the Tools for Success: Adult Education Centers

Adult Education Centers are a central component of the RET centers. Parents attend alternative high schools, obtain tutoring in a variety of subjects and participate in literacy and intergenerational activities with their children. Adult education is presented in the context of family literacy and parenting skills so that young mothers build literacy skills in a relevant, meaningful setting and so that they begin to view learning as a lifelong process. Like our other parental programs these centers are based on the notion that to encourage and advance parents' education is to nurture family education and, therefore, family success.

At the Alternative High Schools located on-site at all four RET centers, teachers licensed by the New York City Board of Education offer classes to students between the ages of 14 and 21. Using the computer centers (equipped with IBM computers with multilevel educational software), group discussion sessions and traditional workbook learning, students who have dropped out of school (both parents and teenage children) can complete their secondary education and prepare for the General Equivalency Diploma exam. Career and employment counseling is also offered and referrals are made to other appropriate HFH programs. Caseworkers and teachers lead field trips to governmental and private agencies to give students an introduction to career options. At the same time, parents at the Alternative High School are often paired with career women in city agencies who serve as mentors and role models to the homeless mothers.

Parents can also choose from an array of other educational programs at the Adult Education Centers. For those who want to learn or improve their English, English as a Second Language courses are taught. Parents can use the flexible computer programs to explore their interests, including word processing or creative writing. College preparatory materials and guidance are also offered. The young mothers participate in literacy exercises and contextual learning through the use of everyday materials and issues, teaching them basic education skills and life skills. For example, students study leases, read housing authority materials and utility bills, inspect food labels for nutritional value, assess community resources and learn how to communicate with their children and their children's teachers.

The Adult Education Centers also provide educational opportunities for the family as a whole. Working with the Child Development Centers, they sponsor reading and literacy activities for both parents and children. These programs apply strategies that directly involve parents in their children's education and development, an educational approach recommended by growing numbers of scholars, especially for parents of at-risk children. Parents and children also take advantage of Child Development Centers' Quiet Reading Corners, each stacked with hundreds of children's books (see Chapter 3). Additionally, parents at the Alternative High School have created Parent-Teacher Associations with the Child Development Centers' staff to provide another forum for the discussion of educational issues regarding their children.[9]

Like most of our programs at HFH, the Adult Education Center benefits immeasurably from its on-site location at the RET center. Research has indicated that a frustrating array of logistical barriers prevent even the most highly motivated low-income parents from participating in such programs. Transportation difficulties, scheduling and lack of adequate child care are among the most common problems.

Alternative High School
1993

*S*elina, 22, values her GED from the Alternative High School more than any of her other accomplishments at Homes for the Homeless. With her two children enrolled in the Jump-Start program, she is able to focus on her own education while her children do the same. "Biology, Algebra, History, English—I've learned about all of them. I've learned about computers, too. I'm very proud of myself. When you come here they give you a lot of options—if you don't have a GED, they offer you the classes. If you want to go to college, they tell you the best and fastest way to get there. They've got everything here. It's all up to you, if you want to do it. It's up to you."

"While I'm learning at the Alternative High School, my kids are also learning at the Child Development Center. My five-year old is writing, and she knows her abc's. My four-year old son is starting to write his name, so by the time he gets to school he'll be ready to take everything in and my daughter will, too."

At the RET centers, however, the services and supports that allow parents to take part in classes are on-site and integrated with other HFH programs.[10]

Learning the Ropes of Everyday Living: The PLUS Program

Another adult-education program at HFH addresses a parent's more practical needs. Because many homeless families today are so young and lack independent living skills, we've developed the Practical Living/Useful Skills (PLUS) program. PLUS seeks to equip adult residents with the information and motivation they will need to handle the challenges involved in raising a family, from securing permanent housing to more basic elements of parenting and managing a household. We cover a broad range of topics to meet parents' diverse needs: apartment maintenance, tenant rights and responsibilities, financial management and more personal issues such as child discipline, domestic violence, self-esteem and substance abuse.

Since PLUS is both a primary-prevention program and a parent-support program, we've structured it around informal and highly interactive workshops. RET center family caseworkers facilitate the workshops, which meet weekly, for six sessions. These caseworkers are key to the success of the program. Because we maintain a high caseworker-to-family ratio of one to 20, the resulting relationship between a parent and her caseworker tends to be close, supportive and trusting. Over the course of their stay at the RET centers, families come to view their caseworker not as a caseworker, but as a neighbor and a friend. This strong relationship plays a critical role in a family's successful participation in HFH programs, including the PLUS programs. PLUS workshop topics are organized into eight areas:

- Parenting, child behavior and child abuse
- Self-esteem and personal relationships
- Domestic violence

- • AIDS/HIV
- • Nutrition
- • Housing and apartment maintenance
- • Budgeting and consumer affairs.

In addition to the housing workshops (see Chapter 6), classes addressing parenting and child development issues are among the most important and most popular. This is not surprising, as many homeless parents feel unsure or defensive about their parenting abilities. For homeless mothers the specter of having their children taken away by city child protective agencies always looms dangerously close (see Chapter 5).

Because parenting is so complex and because homeless parents face such difficult and unique challenges, PLUS workshops strive, above all, to be supportive and flexible. Instructors begin by reassuring parents that they, not the government nor anyone else, are the experts on their children and the most important people in their children's lives. Mothers learn about specific parenting skills and the dynamics of the parent-child relationship, while also discussing their own experiences. And although participants tend to represent a range of experiences and needs, this very diversity often enriches the workshops. Indeed, we have found that some of the most valuable learning in the sessions takes the form of peer and parent-to-parent exchanges.

Workshop coordinators structure each session around the individual parent's needs, questions and interests. Recognizing the varied ways people learn and participate, the staff draws on many techniques, including working in small and large groups, watching videos, role playing, writing and drawing. By the final sessions, parents begin teaching and leading the workshops. In the process, they not only learn about parenting, but also build broader skills of confidence, leadership and planning. As many scholars have found, this participant-directed,

Island RET Center

1993

At 23, Sonya looks more like a young girl than the mother of two preschoolers. At 15 she began experimenting with crack and soon became addicted. Eventually she was forced to leave her children with her mother and take to the streets.

"I was sleeping on the streets, and I had friends who robbed people for money to buy drugs. I landed in jail and a man there told me if I didn't get off the streets, I'd be sent to Rikers Island Prison. I learned my lesson right there. I said to myself, 'I gotta get off this stuff, because this isn't me.'"

Now living at the Island RET center, Sonya is focusing on herself and her children—the entire family attends the educational programs offered there. In addition, Sonya finds extra support from the PLUS workshops. "I go to the parenting workshops for my son and daughter to learn how to take care of them. I don't want to abuse my kids. When I get stressed out, I go to the workshops and talk about things with the other mothers. By talking things through and stepping back a minute, I can cope much better."

"I love my children very much. I want to be a kind mother and be open—something I didn't have. But I'm learning to be that way for my kids."

collaborative approach—whereby the staff serves not as experts, but as facilitators—is key. When parents are homeless and, therefore, at risk of losing their sense of parental authority, such an approach is particularly critical (see Chapter 2).[11]

Over 100 residents attend at least one PLUS workshop each week, with roughly 500 individuals graduating from the six-week PLUS series each year. Upon successful completion of each workshop, RET center staff hosts celebrations and presents participants with PLUS graduation certificates that, in turn, serve as supporting documentation for housing applications, landlord interviews, job training and other programs. In addition, parents are encouraged to continue learning about the workshop topics on their own. At the end of each parenting workshop, for example, the staff provides lists of other parenting courses offered at hospitals, day-care centers and community organizations throughout New York City.

From Welfare to Work: The Employment Training Program

For many homeless families, securing a long-term job is the ultimate hurdle. Despite negative media portrayals and misinformed public opinion of families dependent on public assistance, most heads of such households would prefer to be economically self-sufficient. A 1990 study of homeless people in 381 shelters across 20 states found that during the previous month, 55 percent had looked for work. Similarly, a survey of homeless parents in a Massachusetts shelter found that 87 percent named a job or career as their major goal or dream in life. Through concrete resources and comprehensive support, RET centers work to make those dreams possible.[12]

While other job-training programs exist, including government programs geared specifically to welfare recipients, most are inadequate for homeless parents (see Table 5). Because they often begin at a much lower job-readiness level, for instance, homeless heads-of-household

TABLE 5: QUALIFICATIONS NEEDED FOR PUBLIC ASSISTANCE RECIPIENTS TO PARTICIPATE IN JOB TRAINING PROGRAMS VS. THE TYPICAL HOMELESS HEAD-OF-HOUSEHOLD

The typical job training program requires that the candidate:	The typical homeless head-of-household:
• have a high school diploma	• has a tenth grade education
• read at an 8th grade level or better	• reads at the 6th grade level
• possess basic skills, such as typing	• has few employable job skills
• provide their own daycare	• has limited access to daycare
• have no substance abuse history	• often has a substance abuse history
• provide their own transportation	• can not afford transportation costs
• read and write English	• may not read or write English
• be job-ready	• has virtually no work experience
• have a permanent address	• does not have a permanent address
Source: Institute for Children and Poverty	

Homeless heads-of-household stand very little chance of succeeding in, or even qualifying for, typical job training programs.

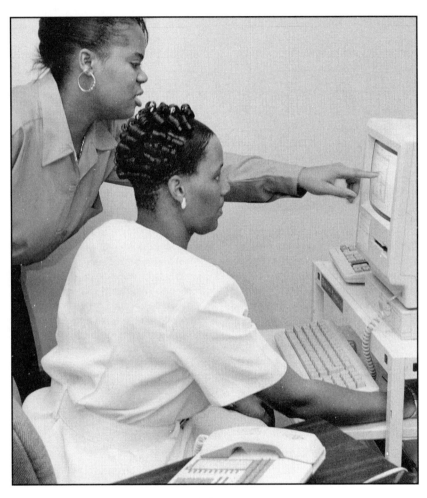

Train And Gain Program
1993

TAG intern Linda, 25, mother of a three-year-old daughter, wrote in an essay for her GED class at the Alternative High School: "The TAG program shows you can reach any goal if you want it bad enough. They are teaching me computers and clerical work — work I never realized I could do and that I would like. This program has helped me realize that I can do something with my life. I chose to make a difference in myself, for myself and my child. Because I believe in gaining, not losing."

require more basic and more intensive education and training than is typically offered. Moreover, many need supportive services unavailable in traditional programs, from child care to assistance with the transition from homelessness to permanent housing. Even those programs geared specifically for homeless people neglect the needs of today's typical homeless family: most are designed for homeless men, single women or the formerly homeless.[13]

HFH developed the Train and Gain (TAG) program to fill this fundamental need for a more appropriate employment program. Building on the other educational and social programs already in place at the RET centers, TAG provides a combination of extended training and guidance tailored to the specific needs of HFH families. The program also furnishes crucial support services, including child care, intensive counseling and job placement. In addition, we designed TAG to accommodate participation in adult literacy and GED programs while learning employment skills both in the classroom and in a work environment. A sequential outline of the TAG program is as follows:

Pre-Employment Workshops. TAG participants attend a pre-employment, week-long workshop before beginning their job training. The workshop helps participants become job ready by addressing such issues as researching and choosing a career, assessing skills, experiences and work-related preferences, writing resumes and cover letters, interviewing and meeting on-the-job performance standards. The workshop gives the participants the opportunity to be self-reflective and to think about their skills and interests, as well as personal issues (childcare needs, substance abuse histories, work and educational experiences) which might influence their employment options. Workshop leaders and participants also discuss the educational, counseling and training options offered at the RET centers, and assess which combination of services is most appropriate for each participant.

Education and GED Preparation. TAG participants without a high school or GED diploma enroll in the RET Centers' Alternative High Schools to prepare for the GED exam. Participants can also take part in basic education and literacy programs to enhance their reading comprehension and general literacy skills. Participation is based on individuals needs; a participant might choose to enroll in GED preparation simultaneously with the TAG program, or she might decide that she needs to concentrate first on passing the GED examination before she can devote time to the TAG program.

Mentoring & Skill-Building Internships. TAG participants may choose to receive employment training in one of the following career fields: child care, social services, security, janitorial services and housekeeping, building maintenance, food service, and clerical work. After they choose a specific career field, participants are matched with employee mentors who work at the participants' RET Center and serve as their instructors for on-the-job training. Participants work side-by-side with their mentors performing the daily tasks associated with a particular job. This initial stage of the TAG program helps participants become accustomed to the requirements of the work environment: punctuality, good attendance, arranging child care, accepting criticism, and taking initiative. In the second, core component of the program, TAG participants are placed in job internships at the RET Centers. Interns are expected to perform job tasks independently and report to supervisors, who provide feedback and performance evaluations.

Practical Living/Useful Skills (PLUS) Workshops.
TAG participants also attend PLUS workshops. These workshops provide instruction on daily living skills such as apartment maintenance, lease negotiation, budgets, and nutrition, and help participants address such personal issues as domestic violence, stress management, and parenting. These workshops, offered to all RET Center residents, provide the skills families need to maintain permanent housing and live independently.

Employment and Basic Skill-Building Workshops.
During their TAG internship, participants attend weekly workshops that provide intensive support and guidance on issues related to working and finding employment. Pertinent topics include making the transition to work, juggling parenting responsibilities and a job, finding affordable daycare, budgeting, conducting a job search and applying for transitional public assistance benefits. In addition, issues that may arise on the job, such as interacting with co-workers, sexual harassment, and employee self-initiative are discussed. A substantial part of each workshop is devoted to enhancing contextual learning through work-relevant training and problem solving. Workshop activities include the following: reading and discussing relevant newspaper articles, typing and word processing practice sessions, writing resumes, and filling out work-related forms.

Job Search and Placement. Once TAG graduates have acquired needed job skills they are placed in permanent, paid positions. Employment opportunities for TAG participants are secured through contacts with the more than 70 vendors, contractors, and organizations with which Homes for the Homeless conducts routine business. In addition, employment searches are conducted through job banks and various other government agencies that provide placement services. TAG graduates also receive assistance with finding employment through the newspaper "help wanted" section. To date **40 percent** of all TAG graduates have found gainful employment in positions that pay between $16,500 and $21,000 annually.

Post-Placement Services. Job placement caseworkers maintain regular contact with participants after they graduate from the program. Caseworkers assist with any problems that could threaten a graduate's new-found employment including poor job performance, child-care problems, transportation difficulties, or health problems. By extending the network of social services established in the RET Centers, caseworkers provide TAG graduates with a valuable resource that can help them to remain employed and housed.

By offering such intensive, comprehensive training and services, TAG provides a more realistic and effective employment program for homeless families. Through TAG, we strive to meet the individual and collective needs of these families. Yet we are also flexible. Participants choose how rapidly they go through the program and the range of skills they want to learn. For the roughly 15 percent of HFH families with minimal needs and problems, TAG furnishes only what they need—freeing caseworkers to provide the extra support services for the many other families who require them.

The TAG program also avoids the fatal shortcomings of previous employment training and placement programs. Numerous studies identify the typical problem of unrealistic expectations and preparation. In other words, many programs do not provide for a changing job market or economic climate and often leave their participants without the flexibility to adapt. More broadly, job training programs often neglect to prepare students for the disappointments of the job search and the rigors of full-time employment.[14]

For homeless parents, however, the biggest obstacle to employment is the lack of support. Training for and obtaining a job is simply not enough for these families, just as housing is not enough. Mounting evidence suggests that job-training and education programs for low-income people, or "welfare-to-work" programs, cannot be widely effective unless we support participants in their personal and family lives. Child care and transitional family income support are among the most important requirements for success and are key to our job training model.[15]

Job training programs that provide family-based support are also more likely to help children. Recent studies have revealed that "welfare-to-work" programs that address the needs of both parents and children not only stand a better chance of success with the parents, who are more highly motivated, but also improve the children's own

Train And Gain Program

1993

Danielle, 24, describes her involvement in the TAG program: "TAG is helping me to learn to do things that I should do, making me realize what's best for me, so that I'll be able to hold down a job. That's why I think the program lasts six months—so you can get into the habit of doing the work you have to do. If you don't want to do it, you can drop out, but I'm not going to be a dropout. I'm going to go on and work in a restaurant for awhile, to keep bread on our table and a roof over our heads. Once my daughter is old enough to go to school, I can think about doing something else, maybe even counseling. The way my life has been, I have a lot to share with other people— my experiences might help them. Not just with drugs but in other areas. I can help people so they don't go down the wrong road."

chances for developing the skills needed to become self-sufficient adults. To succeed as a "two-generation" program, however, it must encompass six key elements:

- family and child need assessment
- quality child care and early education
- parenting support services
- preventative health services
- employment training and services
- case management and follow-up.[16]

In conjunction with other RET center programs—Child Development Centers, PLUS workshops, health care—TAG offers all of these necessary components, while providing the additional intensive supports often needed by homeless parents seeking employment. That all of this is offered on-site and for extended periods means additional benefits for parents and children. The TAG program is accessible, coordinating with other services, and flexible, working around family needs.

Finally, for many RET center residents, TAG inspires. As they watch their peers progress through the program, leave public assistance and obtain jobs that truly support their families and hold future promise, many HFH parents say they gain hope. In addition, those TAG graduates now working at the RET centers often serve as mentors and role models, embodying the potential for successfully moving out of homelessness and poverty.

THE RESULTS

The parent-education programs at HFH form a framework that supports not only the individual adult, but also the entire family. Strengthening parents' educational, employment and life skills enables them to nurture, support and guide their children. And, like all HFH programs, we developed the parent programs to solidify the foundation of the family and provide the opportunity for parents and children to build healthy independent lives. The results are impressive:

Alternative High School Results

In the past four years, over 200 mothers have graduated from the Alternative High School's GED preparation courses and 80 percent of those taking the exam passed on the first try. Many mothers go on to pursue junior college or college educations, while others enroll in either TAG or another employment program.

The educational growth of a parent most noticeably affects a child. Students at the Alternative High School are more than three times as likely to be in contact with their children's teachers; more than 90 percent of mothers who are working toward their GED have stated the primary reason for doing so was "to set an example for my children."

PLUS Program Results

The success of this program is reflected not only in the sheer number of participants, but also in the impact the workshops have on parents' ability to maintain independent lives once placed in permanent housing.

Approximately 86 percent of all residents attend at least two PLUS workshops during their stay at an RET center, with 73 percent graduating from the six-week series of workshops. The topics covered in the PLUS workshops play a key role in the most encouraging results of all: that roughly *94 percent* of families who have lived at HFH's RET centers have remained in their original permanent housing placement for at least two years. While HFH's PLUS INC aftercare program (see Chapter 6) provides a continuum of support services, it is the independent living skills learned in the PLUS workshops that enable families to make the transition from shelter life to their own apartments.

TAG Program Results

As a pilot program over the past 18 months, TAG has shown encouraging results. The goals for the first year of TAG were based on realistic expectations measured against the performance targets of other job-training and placement programs. Of the 40 parents who participated in TAG in the past year:

- 75 percent graduated from the TAG program
- 61 percent found employment
- 18 percent went on to further their education
- 12 percent were actively seeking employment
- 8 percent continued in internships.

Now as an established program, we plan to recruit and train roughly 600 participants over the next three years.

As is our policy with all new programs, we will continue to monitor TAG and modify it as results and client feedback are analyzed. Our philosophy of family preservation, support and education is the foundation upon which all of the programs are built, thus ensuring that the individual programs provide continuity and reinforcement throughout.

Yanick, Brunetta and Shore
1993

KEEPING FAMILIES TOGETHER AND HEALTHY:

Prevention and Preservation Programs

Homeless families regularly confront problems that threaten not only the well-being of individual family members, but also the very cohesion of the families themselves. Often lacking the resources to prepare or protect themselves, they become consumed by the difficult physical and mental health problems common to homelessness and poverty. Many times families that become homeless *already* bear the scars of a past filled with violence, instability and neglect. However, because they are homeless, their chances for relief and treatment are slimmer than ever. In fact, such problems may cause the break-up of a homeless family.

Like so much of homeless policy, the response to the health problems, child abuse and neglect that endanger homeless families is inadequate. In some ways it is even harmful. Although many programs strive to prevent and treat problems such as substance abuse and depression, their scope is too limited and their methods are often inappropriate for homeless families. Furthermore, existing child-welfare policy often punishes homeless parents too severely and prematurely for having such problems. Indeed, homeless parents risk losing their children simply by *being* homeless; the lack of a stable home is frequently interpreted as neglect.

Because these realities threaten to tear apart homeless families, we believe that families should be offered support in preserving and strengthening themselves. We know the harm poverty and homelessness alone can do; taking more and more children away from their parents and placing them in the overcrowded foster care system only adds to the damage families have already sustained. At HFH, therefore, we make family preservation and foster care prevention central goals. While virtually all RET center programming is family-based, we created several special programs that work toward these objectives specifically. From preventative health care to the respite of a crisis nursery, our programs give homeless families the critical support they need to stay healthy and to stay together.

THE RATIONALE

Homelessness (and the severe poverty associated with it) carries a variety of physical, emotional and social miseries for families. Chronic poor health among children is particularly common. For a variety of reasons, homeless children tend to suffer from even more health and nutritional problems than poor children do. As one medical expert has put it, "if poverty is bad for children's health, homelessness is little short of disastrous." Homeless children suffer disproportionately from nutritional deficiencies, growth problems, upper respiratory infections, skin and ear disorders, gastrointestinal problems, lice infestations and chronic physical disorders. Furthermore, homeless families overutilize emergency room services, underutilize preventative health services, and have far fewer dental visits.[1]

Homeless children are also prone to emotional and behavioral disorders. Depression and anxiety also afflict such children to a much greater extent than they do non-homeless children. In one study, over half of the homeless children surveyed needed psychiatric evaluation and one-third were clinically depressed. Behavioral disturbances also occur with unsurprising frequency. Typical problems include increases in fighting, restlessness, aggression, shyness, withdrawal, sleeping difficulties or trouble concentrating.[2]

Homeless parents are also at higher risk of physical and mental illness and, more commonly, emotional problems. With its daily trauma, uncertainty and painful deprivations, homelessness produces profound feelings of sadness and hopelessness in people of all ages, emotions that often lead to severe clinical depression.[3]

Substance abuse problems also plague growing numbers of homeless families. In fact, substance abuse now ranks as the most prevalent health problem among the homeless. Although little data exists for families in particular, the percentage of homeless adults suffering from alcoholism or alcohol abuse is generally estimated at 30 to 40 percent. Other drug abuse, including cocaine and heroin, affects between 10 and 15 percent of homeless individuals, although some studies report prevalence rates as high as 70 percent. Overall, the incidence of substance abuse among the homeless is estimated to be at least three to six times greater than that of the general population. At HFH in 1992, over *two-thirds* of heads-of-household had some form of alcohol or drug problem (see Figure 20). Fewer than half had received treatment before coming to our RET centers.[4]

These and other problems often lead homeless parents to neglect and physically abuse their children. In New York City, the Child Welfare Administration reports that over one-third of all homeless parents have an open case for abuse or neglect of their children. With too few family-preservation and abuse-prevention services, the city is forced to remove children from their families and placed them in foster care. The foster care population in New York State overall has exploded in

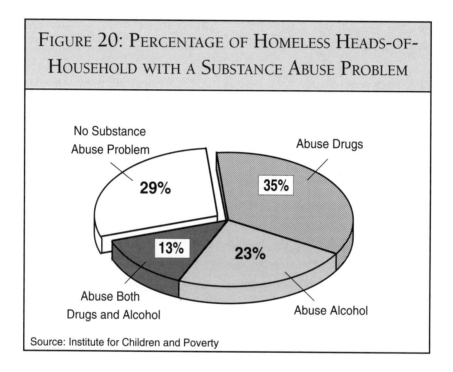

FIGURE 20: PERCENTAGE OF HOMELESS HEADS-OF-HOUSEHOLD WITH A SUBSTANCE ABUSE PROBLEM

No Substance Abuse Problem

Abuse Drugs

29%

35%

13%   23%

Abuse Both Drugs and Alcohol

Abuse Alcohol

Source: Institute for Children and Poverty

Between 1986 and 1988, the number of child abuse and neglect cases, resulting from parents with a substance abuse problem, increased 224 percent in NYC. In 1992, 71 percent HFH heads-of-household had a history of substance abuse.

the past five years, with 25,000 new children entering the system between July 1988 and July 1990 alone. By the end of 1990, the number of children in foster care nationally stood at 71,000, and by December 1992 that number had reached an unprecedented high of 85,800. In less than a decade, New York City witnessed similar dramatic trends in its foster care caseload—from just under 17,000 children in the city's system in 1985 to over 50,000 in 1993 (see Figure 21).[5]

As the numbers continue to increase, the correlation between child abuse and substance abuse becomes more clear, as does the vicious cycle to which parental drug abuse condemns many children. A 1989 study found that 52 percent of children placed in foster care in New York City had a drug-abusing parent. Moreover, drug abuse was the major barrier to family reunification in New York 39 percent of the time. Perhaps most troubling is the fact that of 223 children who entered the city's foster care system in 1986, only 38 percent from drug-abusing families had been placed in permanent homes by the end of 1990. This is in contrast to children from drug-free families, 54 percent of whom found permanent homes in the same time span.[6]

To understand this phenomenon, one must consider the growing number of homeless parents who themselves experienced abuse as children. In a Michigan study of families at risk of out-of-home placement, over 40 percent of the mothers reported that they had been abused or neglected when they were children. At our RET centers, nearly *one third* of the mothers reported they had been physically or sexually abused as children (see Table 6). Many of these women continue to be involved in abusive relationships as adults, worsening the already precarious situation for their children and themselves. As is the case with child abuse, the proportion of homeless women who have suffered from domestic violence is probably underreported. Even so, nearly half of all homeless women say that they have suffered from domestic violence. Numerous studies show that homeless women are twice as likely to be abused and beaten as non-homeless poor women.[7]

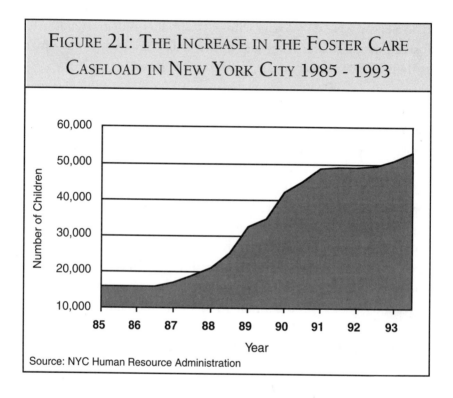

FIGURE 21: THE INCREASE IN THE FOSTER CARE CASELOAD IN NEW YORK CITY 1985 - 1993

Source: NYC Human Resource Administration

In 1985 there were 17,000 children in foster care in NYC; today there are over 50,000—nearly three times as many in less than a decade.

TABLE 6: FREQUENCY OF CHILDHOOD DISRUPTIONS AMONG HOMELESS HEADS-OF-HOUSEHOLD

Disruption	Percent
Physically or Sexually Abused	30%
Lived in Foster Care	20%
Lived in a Single-Parent Household	62%
Parents Divorced	32%
Death of a Parent	24%

Source: Institute for Children and Poverty

Early childhood disruptions are common among homeless heads-of-household—30 percent were physically or sexually abused as children; 20 percent were placed into foster care; and 62 percent came from single parent families.

The tragic corollary to such abuse and neglect of homeless women is, increasingly, the child welfare system's swift assumption of custody of their children. Homeless families run a particularly high risk of such intervention. HFH found that *one in every five* families residing in its facilities had children in foster care. And *one in every three* families residing in our facilities was actively monitored for child abuse by New York City's Child Welfare Agency. In contrast, among U.S. families, only 1 percent have children in foster care.[8]

That disproportionate numbers of homeless children are being absorbed into the child welfare system does not necessarily mean that homeless families are correspondingly more violent or abusive. In fact, most homeless children placed in state custody are deemed neglected (see Figure 22). And what constitutes neglect today encompasses a wide range of complicated circumstances. Neglect, as it is currently defined, also covers problems that are part of, or have been caused by, homelessness itself. Parents, in effect, often lose their children for reasons beyond their control. For example, homeless children are frequently considered medically neglected after their chronic health and emotional problems go untreated. Yet they have often developed these problems because of the nutritional and environmental deprivations endemic to homelessness, not because of a lack of parental concern or diligence. And treatment is lacking because, as noted above, homeless people in the United States have little or no access to healthcare.[9]

Similarly, child welfare officials may cite homeless parents for neglect on the basis of a lack of supervision that is, above all, a by-product of homelessness or the effort to escape it. In order to look for work or housing, homeless parents may have to leave their children unattended. The primary reason: a lack of affordable child care. Inadequate care of children may also stem from a parent's own struggle with depression or illness, again problems caused by the stresses of

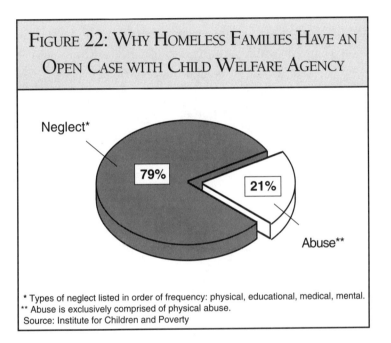

FIGURE 22: WHY HOMELESS FAMILIES HAVE AN
OPEN CASE WITH CHILD WELFARE AGENCY

Neglect*

79%

21%

Abuse**

* Types of neglect listed in order of frequency: physical, educational, medical, mental.
** Abuse is exclusively comprised of physical abuse.
Source: Institute for Children and Poverty

While the majority of open Child Welfare Agency cases among homeless families at HFH are due to neglect, one in every five is the result of abuse.

homelessness. Exhausted and overwhelmed by the relentless fight to provide the very basics for their family, homeless parents may no longer possess the physical or emotional strength to provide for their children's additional needs.[10]

Perhaps the most distressing consequence of homelessness, however, is the break-up of families simply because they are homeless. A New Jersey study found that homelessness precipitated nearly half of all out-of-home placements by the state and 25 percent of those made by Newark. A recent survey of homeless families in New York City is even more striking: over one-third of the families requesting emergency shelter from the city had been separated from at least one other family member because the family had no home of its own. Such separations often result from shelter system regulations—many shelters do not accept older children or a mother's male partner.[11]

Protecting Family Health & Strength: The Need for Prevention and Preservation

Alternatives to the destructive break-up of families are critically needed. Like all Americans, today's homeless children and their parents deserve to have their families supported, yet current policy largely denies them fundamental support services. Furthermore, in the process, our government may very well be crippling future generations; growing evidence suggests that out-of-home placement and homelessness may be linked in a disturbing cycle. And, in addition to the staggering emotional and social cost of family break-up, the financial cost is equally massive, totaling up to $160,000 for each child's stay in the foster care system.

Researchers have long recognized that substitute (foster or group home) care and poverty are linked. After all, the majority of children in state custody are poor. It also appears that as more homeless children enter the protective care system, increasing numbers are "aging out" of that system and, with little chance to learn to live independently, joining the ranks of the new generation of homeless families. HFH research has also found a striking illustration of this circuit between out-of-home placement and homelessness. First, we discovered that the number of homeless parents that grew up in foster, group or residential care had increased dramatically in the late 1980s. Homeless heads-of-household in 1991 were *four* times more likely to have lived in substitute care than their predecessors in 1987. In addition, those individuals with foster care histories became parents at a younger age and had more children. They were also more likely to have been pregnant or to have had newborn children in the year prior to becoming homeless.[12]

Even more troubling, the data suggested that these families also tended to be more unstable than other homeless families, to be struggling with more problems. In fact, the results hint at a new kind of generational cycle (see Table 7). HFH found that homeless parents who had grown up in substitute care were almost twice as likely as parents with no such history to see their *own* children placed into the system. They were also twice as likely to have active cases for child abuse with the Child Welfare Administration. Moreover, they suffered even more substance abuse, domestic violence and mental health problems than the general population of homeless families, putting their families at even greater risk of out-of-home placement.[13]

Although the reason why out-of-home placement often leads to such problems is unclear, most likely it involves the tumult and isolation that pervades so much of the system. Homeless children, whose lives are *already* characterized by instability and loss, seem to be particularly vulnerable when placed in foster care. Forced to adjust to new people, new environments and new schools, they lose the sense of stability and continuity associated with family that is critical to healthy development. Their sense of control is further eroded by the

TABLE 7: PROFILE OF HOMELESS PARENTS WITH A HISTORY OF FOSTER CARE VS. PARENTS WITHOUT A HISTORY

Characteristics	History of Foster Care*	No History of Foster Care
Average Age of Parent	22	25
Age Had First Child	18	20
Children		
Average Number of Children	3	2
Pregnant/Recently Gave Birth	60%	47%
Have Children in Foster Care	27%	15%
Have Active Case with CWA**	73%	29%
Social Welfare Indicators		
Substance Abuse History	79%	60%
Domestic Violence History	60%	41%
Mental Illness History	18%	8%
Housing History		
Previously Homeless	49%	19%
Employment/Welfare History		
Have 6 Mos. Work Experience	18%	45%
Age Began Receiving AFDC	18	21
No. of Yrs. Receiving AFDC	4	2.5

* Homeless parent lived in a foster home as a child
** NYC Child Welfare Administration
Source: Institute for Children and Poverty

Homeless parents who grew up in foster care are significantly younger, have a greater number of children, and are more likely to exhibit a number of social and economic problems in comparison to homeless parents who do not have a history of foster care. Moreover, almost 75 percent of these parents have an open case with the Child Welfare Administration for child abuse and neglect, and nearly twice as many have had their own children placed in foster care.

frequent moves between foster families, and the infrequent contact they have with caseworkers and biological families.[14]

In a sense, homeless children placed in state custody are dealt a double blow: they lose their homes, and then they lose their families. Moreover, the very problems created by the first hardship are compounded by the second. As discussed in Chapter 3, children who experience homelessness run an exceptionally high risk of developmental, educational and emotional problems. Out-of-home care appears only to exacerbate these problems. For example, our staff has observed that the reactive behaviors homeless children already exhibit with their biological parents—such as hyperactivity, violence, and sullen and withdrawn behaviors—tend to worsen when the children go into foster care.

Through several specialized programs, we have found that providing homeless families with crucial intervention services like family counseling, preventative physical and mental health care, and substance abuse treatment in the context of a transitional housing facility can be extremely important in the effort to preserve and strengthen families. It can even be cost-effective. Moreover, this work can be accomplished on-site while children are protected from harm, but not separated from their families. The danger, not the child, is removed.

THE COMPONENTS

After observing first-hand the far-reaching effects of the separations and related problems experienced by increasing numbers of homeless families, HFH developed several programs aimed at prevention and family preservation. We begin with one of the most crucial issues facing homeless children and parents: family health care, including prenatal care and immunization services. Other HFH initiatives include the Family Crisis Nursery, for children at risk of abuse or neglect; the Family Preservation and Reunification Program, to reunite families with children in foster care; and the Together In

Emotional Strength (TIES) program, to address the interrelated problems of substance abuse and foster care. All of these programs are part of a coordinated effort to keep families intact and prevent the debilitating problems that make homelessness difficult to endure, let alone escape.

The Most Essential of Needs: Preventative Health Care Programs

Basic health care is available each day at all four HFH RET centers. In collaboration with community health care providers, on-site registered nurses provide care, complete assessments and make off-site referrals. Doctors from area hospitals visit the RET centers weekly or bi-weekly to provide immunizations, screening tests, physical exams, acute illness care, health education and referrals.

Out of a great necessity, more and more of the health care services offered are for prenatal care. Nearly one-half of the women at HFH are either pregnant or have recently given birth. In 1991, 62 percent of the pregnant mothers who arrived had not received any prenatal care. On-site nurses and visiting doctors now provide more prenatal care and counseling for these expectant mothers as well as for the young and often inexperienced new mothers. The Island RET center in particular specializes in the needs of young mothers: a full-time doctor and nurse are on hand to provide care for expectant mothers.

Since maintaining good health is an extremely important aspect of HFH's overall program, health education at the RET centers focuses on prevention. Although the concept of prevention is often one of the most difficult to convey to young mothers, it is the safest, most inexpensive and most effective method of health care. Our caseworkers work with a variety of health-care providers to teach mothers the basic concepts of healthy living. Workshops cover such topics as hygiene, nutrition, immunizations, reproduction, AIDS and sexually transmitted diseases, stress management and exercise.

Health-care education is not limited to mothers. Young children begin learning about health and hygiene at the Child Development Center through basic routines such as washing their hands before eating. The Healthy Living Centers teach school-age and teen children the importance of proper nutrition and exercise. Rap sessions and informal discussions are also held to explore the complex issues these children face early on, such as self-esteem, sexuality, birth control, sexually transmitted diseases and AIDS.

A Necessary But Temporary Separation: The Prospect Family Crisis Nursery Program

The Crisis Nursery model, which has evolved over the last decade in communities across the United States, was created to prevent child abuse and neglect by giving parents a respite from their children during times of extreme stress and upheaval. Having witnessed the prevalence of child abuse, we've adapted this model for homeless families. In May 1992, we established a Family Crisis Nursery at the Prospect RET center in the South Bronx. Designed as a therapeutic child development center for children under the age of six, it provides respite, security and care. The nursery, which operates 24 hours a day, seven days a week, allows parents to leave their young children for up to 72 hours per visit, up to 30 days per year, and requires no legal separation. Although its primary purpose is to serve homeless families, the Prospect Family Nursery is also open to the entire community.

The primary reasons for nursery use are noted in Figure 23. Some parents may simply need time away from their children in order to cope with the stresses associated with poverty. Others may be ill and need to go to the hospital. Still others may have to attend an overnight substance-abuse treatment program. Professional staff at the nursery identify and respond to such issues by offering counseling and referrals to address the underlying problems that put

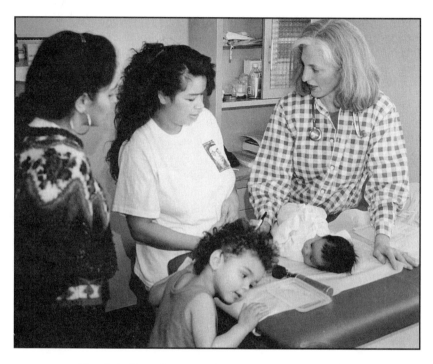

Health Services at Saratoga RET Center

1993

"I had no idea how to take care of my baby—when I had my daughter, I knew I loved her but I was scared, I couldn't understand why she wouldn't stop crying. When I took her to the nurse for her shots, the nurse also showed me how to hold her, how to feed her, and take care of her. Now I know what to do when she cries."

— Maria, 19

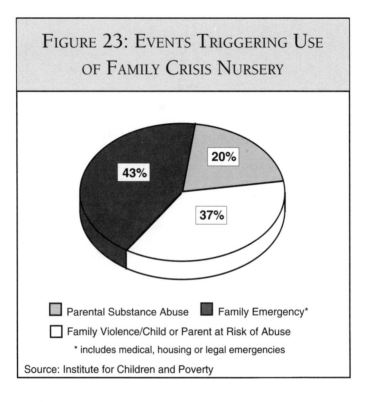

FIGURE 23: EVENTS TRIGGERING USE
OF FAMILY CRISIS NURSERY

20%

43%

37%

■ Parental Substance Abuse   ■ Family Emergency*

□ Family Violence/Child or Parent at Risk of Abuse

* includes medical, housing or legal emergencies

Source: Institute for Children and Poverty

A majority (57 percent) of the parents using the Crisis Nursery report that the underlying reason or triggering event for using the nursery is violence in the home or their own substance abuse problem.

children at risk. Under normal circumstances, children in these neglectful or potentially abusive situations would be placed in foster care. The temporary nature of the Family Crisis Nursery, however, stresses nonlegal action and the preservation of the family. Its primary strategy: to alleviate the pressures threatening the child and thereby avoid a premature and unnecessary initiation of the foster care process.

Children admitted to the nursery are assessed for medical or special developmental needs by a staff that includes child-care workers, teachers and an intervention specialist. While in the nursery, children engage in activities and games that are both educational and specifically geared toward building their self-esteem, trust and sense of control. When necessary, referrals are made to community organizations for the provision of counseling, day care and future medical care for the children.

Because foster care placement almost always occurs in a state of emergency, the nursery acts as a critical buffer for families who lack basic social supports. Given this "time out," parents are free to address whatever family crisis has arisen. The nursery staff also works with the parents, providing on-site educational services, short-term counseling or community referrals.

Also critical to the success of the Prospect Family Crisis Nursery are the follow-up and in-home components. When families pick up their children from the nursery, an aftercare worker makes home visits and linkages to community programs. A 24-hour hotline is also available to assure parents that someone is always there to help and support them. By maintaining strong contact with families and by monitoring their subsequent progress, the aftercare staff provides a continuing support network.

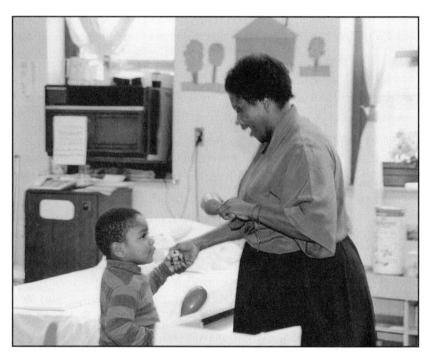

Prospect Family Crisis Nursery
1993

Emergencies *often force families to rely on the Prospect Family Crisis Nursery to avoid foster care placements. Concourse House for Women and Children referred the Gomez family to the nursery when Mrs. Gomez had to be hospitalized for severe depression—putting the family at risk of losing their son, Anthony, to foster care.*

The Director of Concourse House sent a letter of thanks to the nursery:

"The Prospect Family Nursery was there at a time when there were no other options for the Gomez family. The fact that the family is homeless and has no family or friends as resources could have resulted in Anthony entering foster care. However, thanks to your agency the unnecessary placement of yet another child into the enormous foster care system was avoided. Keep up the good work and continue to work towards making a difference in the lives of so many families."

Bringing Families Together: The Family Reunification and Preservation Program

Due to the alarming number of homeless families living at the RET centers with either children in foster care (18 percent) or with open Child Welfare Administration cases (38 percent), HFH recently piloted a program specifically targeted to those families. Working in tandem with our other family-preservation services, the Family Reunification and Preservation program was designed to reunify homeless families with children in foster care and prevent the placement of children into the foster care system.

HFH's Family Reunification Specialist carries out this goal by creating a family-reunification plan with specific objectives and timelines for each family wishing to be reunited with a child in foster care. The specialist, working with a small caseload of four to six families, assists parents by coordinating with the Child Welfare Agency and other members of HFH staff—including Prospect Family Nursery, day care and drug counseling staffs—to provide support and linkages to outside services. Families who have moved into permanent housing are often the most prepared to be reunited with children. Consequently, the specialist also works closely with a family's PLUS INC aftercare worker (see Chapter 6) to ensure the smooth transition of services, making home visits with the aftercare staff as necessary.

Treating the Family as a Whole: The TIES Program

Like the Crisis Nursery, the Together in Emotional Strength (TIES) program attempts to intervene and treat the interrelated aspects of a family problem—in this case, substance abuse—while keeping the family together. The TIES program approaches drug and alcohol abuse problems comprehensively, by simultaneously providing substance abuse treatment and counseling, family support services, education and follow-up services. And, like other RET center programs, the TIES staff works together to tailor its services to the specific needs of each family. This team approach maximizes the network of support for each family.

TIES is holistic and intensive. As soon as they enter the program, parents *and* their children meet with a caseworker who works with them daily on all issues likely to exacerbate the parent's substance abuse problem. A caseworker-to-family ratio of one to 10 ensures the quality of this relationship. Families also participate daily in a substance abuse treatment program that not only works to eliminate the parent's chemical dependency, but allows her to evaluate the various ways in which drugs affect family life. Through additional group-therapy sessions and workshops, parents work on managing stress, modifying negative behaviors and improving their parenting skills. Off-site, outpatient rehabilitation for participants is also available if necessary (see Figure 24).

Because family preservation is key, children participate as an integral component of the TIES program. Unlike many traditional substance-abuse treatment programs, TIES works with children to address the emotional wounds incurred through the abuse. Children learn to share feelings and experiences through family counseling and discussion groups. Caseworkers also encourage them to explore related issues of child abuse, family violence and homelessness, helping children understand that their family's problems are not their fault and that other children deal with the same emotional burdens. At the same time, they participate in educational programs to enhance their self-esteem and decision-making skills.

Because families are living on-site, participation in these programs produces minimal disruption. This is particularly important for homeless children, who are already vulnerable to feelings of instability and loss. In addition, the RET center's family-based case management

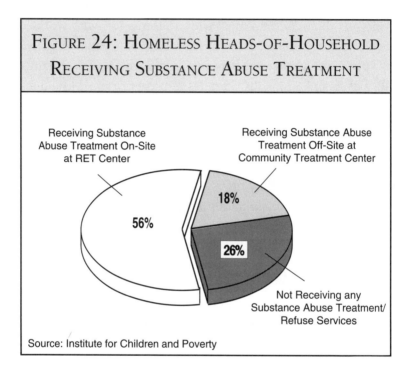

FIGURE 24: HOMELESS HEADS-OF-HOUSEHOLD
RECEIVING SUBSTANCE ABUSE TREATMENT

Receiving Substance
Abuse Treatment On-Site
at RET Center

Receiving Substance Abuse
Treatment Off-Site at
Community Treatment Center

18%

56%

26%

Not Receiving any
Substance Abuse Treatment/
Refuse Services

Source: Institute for Children and Poverty

*Over half of the RET center families with a substance abuse history
received treatment services on-site.*

means that caseworkers already enjoy a close, trusting relationship with families and know their individual needs and strengths. As a result, potential problems can be detected early on and thorough, supportive solutions worked out before trouble escalates to the point where more drastic (and more permanent) intervention might be necessary. Furthermore, caseworkers, child-care workers, and others involved with the family work as a team to ensure that other family needs, such as the children's education, are not endangered during participation in the programs.

THE RESULTS

Though our family preservation programs are relatively new, we have already seen encouraging results. In the first year of operation, the Prospect Family Nursery served over 250 children from 100 families. We anticipate serving almost 500 children in 1993—a 100 percent increase over the pilot year, which indicates the grave need for this service. In addition, we are expanding our services by opening a second Family Crisis Nursery at the Clinton RET center in Manhattan, which will accommodate an additional 150 children annually. The Family Preservation and Reunification program has successfully kept 14 troubled families intact and reunified 10 families in the first 10 months of operation. And in 1992, approximately 100 families including more than 400 children, participated in the TIES program.

As other service providers and researchers have found, proactive family programs are both cheaper and more effective than reactive programs. Clearly, foster care placement is the least desirable solution. The cost of placing a child in foster care can run from $13,000 per year in a foster home to over $40,000 per year in a group home. With the average length of stay at 39 months, each child who enters this system can cost the public $42,000 to $160,000 per stay. While steep, these figures do not begin to reflect the costs incurred by the judicial system to remove a child from his or her family—much less reunite the child with them. By contrast, the annual cost of preventing a child from entering foster care through the intervention of the Family Crisis Nursery is approximately $1,250—a small price to pay when considering the long-term fiscal and social costs of an average foster care stay.[15]

Since we anticipate serving 500 children per year in the Prospect Family Nursery, the net savings to the public could be $6.5 to $20 million annually, depending on the type of foster care placement prevented. By expanding the nursery model to accommodate the roughly 2000 homeless children estimated to be at risk of abuse or neglect in the city, replicated programs could save the city between $26 and $80 million a year.

The TIES program, because of its intensive services, costs more but could have an equally profound impact on family preservation. At an annual cost of roughly $5,000 per child we could save $8,000 to $35,000 by helping a single family prevent a foster care placement. Serving 100 families through TIES could save $1 million annually. This savings could be redirected to support additional prevention programs (see Table 8).

Taken together in their first year of operation, the Prospect Family Nursery and TIES programs may have prevented over 350 children from entering the foster care system, with a financial savings of $6 million and a social and emotional savings that cannot be measured. And, developed in tandem with other on-site services these programs can transform shelters into places where families can stay together.

TABLE 8: ANNUAL COST OF FOSTER CARE PREVENTION VS. COST OF FOSTER CARE PLACEMENT, NYC

| | Preventative Placement | | Foster Care Placement | |
Cost per Child:	Crisis Nursery	TIES	Private Home	Group Home
1 Child	$1,250	$5,000	$13,000	$40,000
100 Children	$125,000	$500,000	$1,300,000	$4,000,000
1,000 Children	$1,250,000	$5,000,000	$13,000,000	$40,000,000

Source: Institute for Children and Poverty

Programs designed to prevent foster care placement offer significant cost savings and have proven effective in the long run.

Branth, Zulma and Dennis

1993

Moving On To Independent Living:

Permanent Housing Programs

For any homeless family, securing a decent, safe home of its own is a desire that transcends all others. More than anything else, these parents long for a house or apartment in which they can live and work independently and where their children can grow up in good health and out of danger. This is a deceptively simple wish. Today, even the educated middle-class that traditionally lived out the "American dream" is finding its most basic elements—a secure career and home ownership—beyond reach. For most poor, undereducated families, that dream is even more elusive.

Homeless families are well aware of the magnitude of this challenge. They know how difficult it is to support a family and a home. They also understand, from painful experience, how alarmingly easy it is to lose both. But success is possible, particularly when families are given the basic tools and support so often missing in poverty. Transitional housing facilities like those operated by HFH are the first step, but continued services and support are critically important.

Unfortunately, most homeless policy stops short of this. Despite the fact that many families return to the shelter system after a temporary stint in what should have been permanent housing, few programs address post-shelter issues. For the most part, families leaving shelters for new homes are simply left to their own devices in already overwhelmed and underserviced communities. Recognizing that the post-placement phase is just as important as the shelter experience, HFH developed a program that provides critical follow-up support.

THE RATIONALE

Many homeless families in the United States enter the shelter system more than once. A 1990 study of families in shelters in southeastern U.S. cities revealed that 60 percent had previously stayed in a shelter two to five times. In New York City, half of the families in the city's shelters have already been through the system at least once before, as noted in Chapter 1. A 1992 study conducted by a research team at New York University found that nearly one-third of the homeless families surveyed had experienced homelessness at least twice. A more recent New York City study demonstrated even higher rates: almost two-thirds of the population requesting emergency shelter had been homeless before.[1]

Based on our past experiences, HFH identified the following factors which increase a family's risk of losing their home a second time:

- Substance abuse
- Domestic violence
- Child abuse and neglect (inadequate parenting skills)
- Medical problems
- Apartment maintenance problems and rent arrears
- Income maintenance problems.

Various reasons account for the high (and growing) rate of recidivism. Rehoused homeless families, already fragile and unstable, are particularly vulnerable. Problems that might otherwise merely require assistance from relatives or a community center may, in the case of a young, isolated family, result in a financial or family crisis, or even another episode of homelessness. The ability to cope is often hampered by still another disadvantage: a growing number of homeless families have never been primary tenants or lived on their own. As Figure 25 indicates, *over half* of the families residing at our RET centers have never lived on their own.[2]

Furthermore, many formerly homeless families are still struggling with the problems that led to their homelessness. Even after extensive residential services in transitional housing, for example, a family may still be grappling with substance abuse or domestic violence. Formerly homeless parents that have found jobs may have lost transitional benefits which enable them to work, such as subsidized child care. And a lack of social supports may still leave them with few people to turn to in an emergency or for the day-to-day support *all* parents need—particularly those raising children alone. In short, even if they have laid the groundwork for independent living, rehoused families face an enormous challenge in putting it to practice.

Ignoring the Next Step: Post-Shelter Policy and Programs

The failure to recognize and address the needs of formerly homeless families is a fundamental flaw in existing policy. Most programs, on the federal and local levels, simply cease working with families once they move out of shelters. Because such families are no longer homeless, the reasoning goes, they are no longer in need. Consequently, programs designed to support formerly homeless families in ways that go beyond housing are practically nonexistent. While the McKinney Act provided for a few demonstration programs, the issue of aftercare was not addressed at the federal level. Slowly, however, federal and state governments are beginning to recognize the importance of follow-up programs and are starting to fund

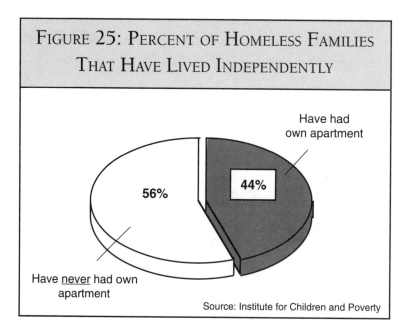

FIGURE 25: PERCENT OF HOMELESS FAMILIES THAT HAVE LIVED INDEPENDENTLY

Have had own apartment

44%

56%

Have <u>never</u> had own apartment

Source: Institute for Children and Poverty

Over half of all homeless families at our RET centers have never lived independently in their own apartment.

new initiatives. For example, New York State has developed the Homeless Rehousing Assistance Program (HRAP) which provides funding for aftercare services directly to non-profits serving formerly homeless families; HFH receives aftercare support money via this program.

In New York City, most aftercare programs operate independent of shelters. That is, when a family leaves a temporary or transitional facility, it is referred to another service provider who furnishes aftercare services exclusively. Although many of these programs are effective, they represent yet another disjointed piece in the fragmented and often uncoordinated services upon which homeless families must build their lives. In addition, the very important aspects of trust and familiarity, crucial to a successful transition and to the provision of aftercare services, are lacking when a family leaves a shelter and is assigned to an outside aftercare provider.

Programs for formerly homeless families run by community-based organizations highlight both the problems and the potential of this approach. Although such initiatives are often successful in helping families stabilize and begin independent lives, their scope is limited. In New York City, where roughly 900 homeless families exit the shelter system each month, only about two dozen programs of this kind are available. As a result, only one-third of eligible families receive such follow up services.[3]

THE COMPONENTS

To ease the transition phase from shelter living to independent living, HFH developed an intensive permanent-housing program. Like all HFH programs, our aftercare service is family-based. We address the specific needs of families who are about to join their new communities (PLUS Housing Workshops), and provide a continuum of in-home aftercare services for families who have moved to a new apartment (PLUS In New Communities–PLUS INC). Bringing it all together is a team of specialists who already enjoy a close, trusting relationship with the families. This feature, more than any other, ensures that the follow-up services are continuous and substantive— perhaps the most important part of a successful transition from homelessness.

Mastering the Basics: Permanent Housing Workshops

Just as today's homeless families need education and job training to secure economic self-sufficiency, so do they often need training in how to obtain and retain a home. Although most of the factors responsible for the shortage of affordable, quality housing are beyond their control, learning about tenant rights, resources and budgeting helps homeless families better respond to any threats to their stability. For that reason, our permanent-housing program begins in the classroom with a series of workshops on navigating today's housing issues.

Shortly after they arrive at our RET centers, homeless families begin preparing for the move to permanent housing. In addition to PLUS workshops (see Chapter 4) that equip parents for independence, two special modules address the specifics of moving, dealing with housing, and raising a family in a new community. A workshop entitled "Unlock the Door" is the first of these. A highly interactive, six-part series, "Unlock the Door" teaches residents how to be their own advocates in the New York City housing market and public-assistance system. Topics include apartment leases, eviction procedures, budgeting, and safety measures.

One of the final workshops RET center residents attend is a series entitled "The Key To Your New Home." Conducted by the same RET center staff members who will later work with families in their new homes, these interactive workshops address an array of issues parents must anticipate and plan for during this transition. The following topics are among those explored:

- Tenant/landlord relationships and rights
- Community resources (education, health care and other services)
- School and child-care registration
- Financial assistance for utilities and phone service
- Developing support networks
- Communicating effectively and assertively.

Since we have found that homeless parents express a considerable range of emotions in response to their transition, workshops address emotional and psychological issues as well. While some participants express a great deal of apprehension, others are overly optimistic, focusing primarily on the freedom and privacy that a new home promises. Through the workshops, parents learn to talk about these feelings and to think realistically but hopefully about the challenges before them. While the benefits of living independently are discussed, for example, so are the fears and isolation that often accompany their newfound "freedom."

Finding a New Home: Housing Placement Programs

After the housing workshops, the search for an apartment begins. To facilitate this complex and often arduous process, housing specialists provide placement assistance in both the public- and private-housing sectors (see Figure 26).

Working individually with RET center residents, our housing specialists find apartments for HFH families, accommodating as best they can the families' needs and community preferences. Unlike many other housing placement programs, our program aggressively targets the private-housing market. Like many other programs, this one began out of frustration and dire need. Too many homeless families

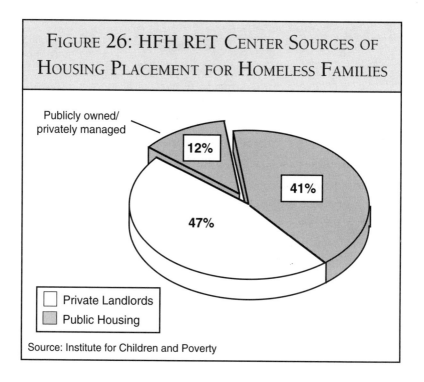

FIGURE 26: HFH RET CENTER SOURCES OF
HOUSING PLACEMENT FOR HOMELESS FAMILIES

Publicly owned/
privately managed

12%

41%

47%

☐ Private Landlords
▨ Public Housing

Source: Institute for Children and Poverty

Almost half of all housing placements at our RET centers are made
through private sources.

were being snared for months in bureaucratic muddles and delays, only to be given housing that was inappropriate, substandard or even uninhabitable. To give them more options and more livable homes, we broadened the housing specialists' search to include privately owned apartments.

The housing specialists began a systematic recruitment and marketing campaign to identify private landlords willing to rent to homeless families. The objectives are twofold: to increase the number of private-sector apartments available and to maintain a low rate of housing loss among families placed in those apartments. By necessity, the program begins by "selling" private owners the idea of renting to homeless families. The unfortunate truth is that many landlords are hesitant to lease to families of any kind, let alone homeless families. Typically, they fear both the high risk that homeless families represent, and the community opposition their presence often sparks. To overcome these attitudes, housing specialists work to educate and assure landlords by helping them obtain government subsidies and providing a commitment of follow-up assistance.

This approach is fairly unusual. Unlike numerous programs that apply strict criteria and thereby end up screening out homeless families, we place even those families exhibiting risk factors such as substance abuse or domestic violence. Housing specialists are able to make these placements primarily because of the work accomplished at the RET centers. Landlords know the kind of services and support families have received and will continue to receive in their new communities through the PLUS INC program.

However, to safeguard against future problems, housing specialists take a series of important preventative steps. They work closely with our family caseworkers and others at the RET centers throughout the placement process. Together, the team makes sure that a family is matched with a landlord and a community that suits its individual needs. Homeless families are often rehoused in unfamiliar or underserved neighborhoods or inappropriate buildings. The results can be disastrous: families may end up abandoning an apartment and eventually becoming homeless again. Placement near their previous residence, in contrast, or near family and other sources of support, goes a long way toward helping families stabilize and maintain long-term independence. We've found that the quality of placement is often as important as the fact that permanent housing has been found at all.

Going the Extra Step: Post-Placement Follow-up Services

Determined to allow families continuous, coordinated services even after homelessness, we've designed our own post-placement program. PLUS INC (Practical Living/Useful Skills In New Communities) is a case-management program that continues the work performed by RET center family services caseworkers. It provides critical follow-up services, such as linking families to community resources and programs, that pick up where HFH services leave off.

PLUS INC begins with consultations between family services caseworkers and PLUS INC fieldworkers just before a family moves to permanent housing. They discuss the family's status and needs using the Needs Assessment Form. Developed in coordination with RET center staff, this process provides information about a family's problems and accomplishments, and determines which services are to be provided by the PLUS INC fieldworker. The PLUS INC staff also meets on their own with each family while they are still in the RET center. Such meetings allow families to get to know the staffperson who will be visiting them in their homes. These meetings also enable fieldworkers to assess the existence or severity of such problems as child abuse, substance abuse, mental and physical health problems, unavailable child care, or a history of rent arrears.

Based on conferences with the family and its family services case-worker, as well as the Needs Assessment Form, the PLUS INC staff places the family in one of three categories: minimal needs, moderate needs or intensive needs. These classifications reflect the diversity of client needs. This tier rating corresponds to the number of risk factors a family faces and determines the average length of time the PLUS INC staff needs to assist them: Intensive Needs families: 12 to 15 months; Moderate Needs: nine to 12 months; and Minimal Needs: six to nine months. Minimal Needs families generally require assistance in the basic moving procedures. Moderate Needs families, in addition to this help, may need extra support and help in addressing building maintenance problems or in accessing child-care, health care or other community services. Intensive Needs families, still facing issues of domestic violence, substance abuse or mental health problems, require more thorough crisis-management services. They also tend to have difficulty paying rent, using community services and securing building maintenance.

Beginning in 1990, HFH experienced a surge in the number of newly housed families classified as Intensive Needs families. Some families are classified as having Intensive Needs when they first come to a RET center, but this classification is reduced to Minimal or Moderate after counseling, services and other programs. However, the unexpected availability of housing and subsequent placements in the early 1990s meant that a homeless family's average RET center stay of six to eight months dropped to three months. That meant families often left the center for permanent housing before their problems had been adequately addressed (see Figure 27).

Once families have settled into their new homes field workers visit them—once a month for Minimal Needs families, twice a month for Moderate Needs families, three to four times a month for Intensive

Independent Living
1993

Former Prospect RET center resident Cheryl, 24, moved with her two young daughters and one son to an apartment in the Bronx. She is currently being supported by welfare, but with the help of her PLUS INC aftercare worker, is locating child care in her new neighborhood so that she can attend a nearby junior college.

Her PLUS INC worker assists in a variety of ways: "People like Cheryl just need that extra little push, an ongoing positive influence that will help them apply the things they learned at the RET center."

"There's a lot of anxiety when a family moves out. Hopefully, what they've learned will have instilled enough confidence and knowledge to return to a community and cope. PLUS INC is like a parent they can call on to help them along."

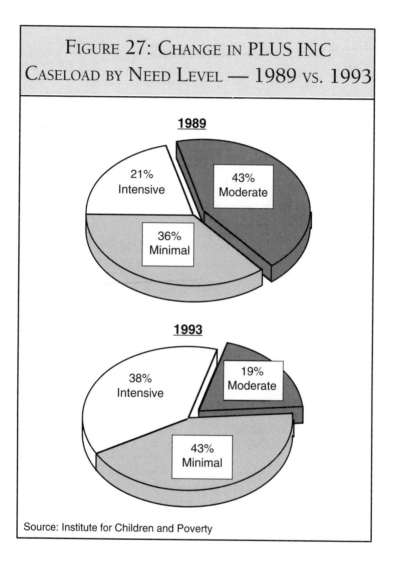

FIGURE 27: CHANGE IN PLUS INC CASELOAD BY NEED LEVEL — 1989 VS. 1993

1989

21% Intensive

43% Moderate

36% Minimal

1993

38% Intensive

19% Moderate

43% Minimal

Source: Institute for Children and Poverty

The number of families requiring intensive follow-up services in permanent housing has almost doubled in the last four years.

Needs families—to monitor their progress and act as a familiar source of support. Most likely, the services and support that the family received at the RET center—free child care, educational support and counseling—are now in short supply. PLUS INC staff work to develop these resources, accompanying families to service providers, government agencies, housing or family courts, domestic violence counseling groups, and medical clinics, as well as routine places like laundromats and grocery stores.

The structure of PLUS INC is key to its success. Each fieldworker is assigned to a specific New York City borough, allowing him or her to become more familiar with local resources, organizations, culture and HFH families in their communities. Fieldworkers also take part in various community meetings, such as city government advisory-board forums and other community events. In addition, the staff works to create support networks composed of former HFH families that live within a building or on the same city block.

The services offered by the PLUS INC program are readily accepted by families for several reasons. First, families view PLUS INC fieldworkers as an extension of the RET center counseling staff. They know the PLUS INC staff is there to continue working with and supporting them. Second, the PLUS INC staff is trained to be community based, differentiating themselves from many other public-sector caseworkers. Third, the staff is very attentive, responding to calls quickly, very often visiting a family on the same day of its request. In addition, if a family requests it, PLUS INC immediately reopens a closed case. Finally, PLUS INC offers concrete and effective services that the families trust the staff to monitor.

THE RESULTS

Since its inception in 1989, PLUS INC has served over 2100 families. Today its caseload numbers approximately 400. Like other components of the RET center model, the PLUS INC program has helped families become truly and permanently independent rather than just temporarily housed. The PLUS INC program simultaneously continues the work begun in the RET center and assists families toward complete independence.

That the program succeeds is evident: Approximately *94 percent* of the families we placed in permanent housing were still residing in their original apartments more than 18 months later. The merits of this comprehensive, family-based continuum of service become particularly obvious when compared to the New York City shelter system's recidivism rate of 50 percent.[4]

"We never imagined when we began that we would make such a difference in so many lives."

— Leonard N. Stern, Founder, Homes for the Homeless

Conclusion

Homes for the Homeless has found that within the daunting challenge of homelessness there exists unparalleled opportunity. This book demonstrates that plausible solutions to the complex issues surrounding family homelessness—education, joblessness, health, family violence, substance abuse, and welfare reform—must be explored if we are to stem the swelling tide of homeless children and their families. By embracing homelessness' comprehensive nature, HFH has piloted innovative programs and services for the past seven years. The Residential Educational Training center model is the product of our research and experimentation. This model offers a bold and coherent approach to family homelessness and a feasible, results-oriented policy alternative.

The imperative to act could not be more compelling. With every day, more and more families fall into the seemingly inescapable cycle of homelessness. Their lives become dominated by a devastating poverty marked by poor education and health, family violence and substance abuse. Yet the greater tragedy underlying all of these issues is that the children, true victims of circumstance, bear the long-lasting effects of homelessness.

Today's homeless children are often the third generation to grow up in extreme poverty. Without a strong policy initiative, we risk having the cycle of homelessness and poverty steal the hopes and dreams of yet another generation of poor children. To rob homeless children of the opportunity to overcome their fears, nurture their talents, and broaden their horizons is to intentionally cripple the future of our country.

In this nation, homelessness serves as a testament to the inconsistent and failed policies of the past. Our government has not provided the necessary leadership to address the plight of family homelessness; simple, poorly executed approaches to homelessness have wasted time and money and have failed to make a difference in the lives of homeless families. To those who propose building more low-income housing as a solution, we argue that this narrow approach ignores the myriad, pressing problems facing young families. To those who advocate cutting welfare and mandating work as a means to welfare reform, we respond that this proposal ignores the many barriers to work faced by homeless heads-of-household: insufficient education, little or no work experience, and the lack of child care options. In response to the vague call to empower homeless families, we believe that the only real way to empower a young, single mother is to provide her and her children with the opportunity to gain skills and education.

This nation must move beyond the present "emergency" mentality when thinking about homelessness and foster a comprehensive, long-term strategy. The Residential Educational Training center model demonstrates the potential of such a strategy. In seven years, thousands of families and their children have walked through our doors, taking with them a renewed sense of hope, another chance to dream, and the promise of a better tomorrow. Still to be tested is the courage and ability of our leaders to face the challenge, and to seize the opportunity. It is not too late to redress a decade of wrongs, and to insure a future for the youngest and most vulnerable families in our society.

Homes for the Homeless believes the solution to homelessness requires leadership and commitment from all levels of government, as well as from the nonprofit and business sectors. Since its founding, our organization has benefited greatly from strong, visionary leadership. We have also had the privilege of collaborating with policy-minded professionals from city, state and federal governments, as well as from the nonprofit, foundation and corporate worlds. This partnership has given us the ability to experiment and to succeed.

In the end, the RET center model is not merely an effective policy option with a sound financial rationale, it is a gateway to a real future for children and their families. No matter how difficult, it is our responsibility as a nation to correct the social deficit and confront the problems of our children. To recall the words of President Lyndon Johnson over thirty years ago, "You don't know the damage poverty can do until you see the scars it can leave on the face of a child who once had a dream." We believe we have developed a model to help erase the scars and restore the hopes, dreams and promise to the children.

APPENDIX I

Methodology

The qualitative data used throughout this book, unless otherwise stated, was obtained from a series of structured interviews and questionnaires conducted by Homes for the Homeless with 596 homeless families residing in HFH's four RET centers throughout 1992. Every family living in each RET center at the time of the study was surveyed. Our survey represents roughly 10 percent of the almost 6000 homeless families living in New York City. All families are referred to our RET centers through the City of New York - Department of Homeless Services and are referred on the basis of room availability. Unlike many shelters, HFH does not exclude any family seeking shelter or screen families through admission criteria. In addition to the structured interviews, HFH routinely tracks the demographics, service needs and progress of all RET center residents. This data, together with a database of information on the more than 7600 families that have been served by the RET centers, is managed by a computer network that links the four RET centers with a central location. Case studies and individual family stories were culled from interviews with the families and HFH staff and from family casenotes. In the stories and quotes, names have been changed to protect the privacy of the children and their families.

Appendix II

A History of Homeless Family Rights Litigation in New York

The following represents a recent history (up until October 1993) of the litigation surrounding family homelessness in New York City. Each prominent case and significant rulings are listed chronologically. The cases listed here were all brought by the Homeless Family Rights Project of The Legal Aid Society.

McCain v. Koch, 70 N.Y. 2d 109 (1987), rev'g in part 117 A.D.2d 198 (1st Dep't 1986):

- Based on the New York State Constitution and statutes, a 1986 Appellate Division and trial court requires the provision of emergency housing to homeless families with children and prohibits the practice of leaving families in City welfare offices overnight.

- A 1987 Court of Appeals decision holds that emergency housing provided to homeless families must meet basic standards of habitability and decency, and that New York State courts have the equitable power to compel compliance. State regulations codifying court orders establish standards for the provision of shelter to homeless families.

McCain v. Koch - continued

Likewise, a 1990 local ordinance bans barracks-style family shelters and prohibits the development of family shelters without self-contained living units, cooking facilities, and adequate living space for each family.

- During the period 1983 to 1989, State and City regulations, as well as agency procedures codifying various trial court interim orders or acceding to relief sought by the plaintiffs are put into place. They include the following: a system for referring families in the shelter system to permanent housing; procedures for ensuring that homeless families are not denied basic public assistance benefits, food stamps and Medicaid as a result of being homeless; procedures for providing notice and an opportunity for an expedited State administrative hearing when shelter is denied or terminated; procedures for providing grants for security deposits and brokers' fees in the actual amounts needed to secure an apartment; procedures to pay storage fees for the duration of a family's homelessness; procedures to issue grants to move possessions when families are transferred among emergency housing placements; and procedures to pay grants to permit families to search for permanent housing.

- A 1989 trial court order prohibits placement of homeless families with children in a welfare hotel that lacks private bathrooms, cooking facilities, and adequate living space for each family, and requires a City remedial plan for referring families placed there to permanent housing or, at a family's option, to alternative shelter facilities. McCain v. Koch, N.Y.L.J., Sept. 22, 1989, at 22, col. 4 (Sup. Ct. N.Y. Co.) (Freedman, J.).

- A June 1990 consent order, inter alia., requires: 1) that the City phase out use of noncompliant welfare hotels and overnight shelter beds; 2) that the City annually provide the necessary amount of permanent housing to homeless families with children so that the combination of temporary and permanent housing is sufficient to meet the need for temporary housing for families; 3) that the City operate at least one 24-hour Emergency Assistance Unit where families can seek shelter; and 4) that the City provide statutory contempt payments, permanent housing referrals, and other remedial relief for 29 named class member families.

McCain v. Koch - continued

- A January 1991 trial court contempt finding against the City of New York is issued based on violations of court orders, including instances where families were kept overnight in City welfare offices or placed repeatedly in unlawful overnight shelter beds, and where families with pregnant women or infant children were placed in barracks-style shelters. McCain v. Koch, N.Y.L.J., Jan. 10, 1991, at 25, col. 6 (Sup. Ct. N.Y. Co.) (Freedman, J.). Subsequently, the City enters into a consent order to provide statutory contempt payments, permanent housing referrals, and other remedial relief to 37 named class member families, and permanent housing referrals and other remedial relief to an additional 22 names class members.

- A 1991 trial court compels compliance with the June 1990 consent order based on the City's failure to end use of noncompliant welfare hotels, including hotels that lack cooking facilities. McCain v. Koch, N.Y.L.J., March 26, 1991, at 24, col. 5 (Sup. Ct. N.Y. Co.) (Freedman, J.); McCain v. Koch, N.Y.L.J., July 3, 1991, at 24, col. 5 (Sup. Ct. N.Y. Co.) (Freedman, J.). The City agrees to withdraw its appeal from these orders after the New York City Council enacted a 1993 local ordinance setting forth a two-year phase out period for noncompliant welfare hotels and adopting the trial court's standard for noncompliance as including hotels that lack cooking facilities.

- November and December 1992 trial court rulings and orders, after extensive contempt hearings, provide the following civil contempt relief based upon ongoing violations of court orders requiring the provision of emergency housing and prohibiting City welfare offices from keeping families there overnight: 1) civil contempt findings against the City of New York, the New York City Human Resources Administration (HRA), and four senior City officials—First Deputy Mayor Norman Steisel, HRA Commissioner Barbara Sabol, HRA Deputy Commissioner Kenneth Murphy, and Jeffrey Carpels, former HRA Executive Deputy Commissioner and current Chief of Staff to Deputy Mayor Cesar Perales; 2) class-wide civil contempt sanctions in the form of a schedule and procedures for providing compensatory payments to class member families who were left overnight in a City welfare office between September 21, 1991 and November 20, 1992; and 3) civil contempt sanctions

McCain v. Koch - continued

against the four senior City officials, in the event that the City did not come into compliance within 30 days, requiring them to be present in a City welfare office on one occasion until homeless families seeking shelter that night were placed in shelter. McCain v. Dinkins, N.Y.L.J., Nov. 24, 1992, at 32, col. 4 (Sup. Ct. N.Y. Co.) (Freedman, J.).

- A July 1993 Appellate Division decision affirms the trial court's orders that: 1) issued civil contempt findings against the City of New York, the Human Resources Administration, and the four senior City officials; and 2) provided compensatory fines to individual class member families. The Appellate Division vacated the sanction requiring the four individual senior City officials to be present at a welfare office on one occasion and remanded the matter to the trial court to impose an appropriate sanction against the individual officials, which the Appellate Division specified could be either a fine or imprisonment. McCain v. Dinkins, N.Y.L.J., Aug. 2, 1993, at 21, col. 3 (1st Dep't 1993).

- An August 1993 trial court decision issued after further hearings makes new civil contempt findings against the City of New York and individual senior City officials First Deputy Mayor Norman Steisel, Deputy Mayor Cesar Perales, HRA Commissioner Barbara Sabol, and Deputy Commissioner Kenneth Murphy for ongoing violations of the welfare office orders from November 20, 1992 through August 3, 1993. The schedule and procedures for providing compensatory payments to class members were extended through August 3, 1993, and the nature of the civil contempt sanction to be imposed on the individual officials is currently sub judice. McCain v. Dinkins, N.Y.L.J., Aug. 6, 1993, at 22, col. 5 (Sup. Ct. N.Y. Co.) (Freedman, J.).

Lamboy v. Gross, 126 A.D.2d 265 (1st Dep't 1987), aff'g 129 Misc. 2d 564 (Sup. Ct. N.Y. Co. 1985) (Freedman, J.):

- A 1987 Appellate Division decision affirms a 1985 trial court order: 1) directing the City to comply with a State administrative directive requiring the immediate provision of shelter to eligible homeless families; and 2) enjoining the State to supervise and enforce compliance. Subsequent enforcement proceedings have been consolidated with McCain.

Slade v. Koch, 135 Misc. 2d 283 (Sup. Ct. N.Y. Co. 1987), modified 136 Misc. 2d 119 (Sup. Ct. N.Y. Co. 1987) (Freedman, J.):

• A 1987 trial court order enforces State regulations and the principles enunciated in State administrative hearing decisions prohibiting the placement of families with pregnant women or children under the age of six months in barracks-style shelter space, and enjoins the State to supervise and enforce compliance. Subsequent enforcement proceedings have been consolidated with McCain.

Barnes v. Koch, 136 Misc. 2d 96 (Sup. Ct. N.Y. Co. 1987) (Tompkins, J.):

• A 1986 trial court order enjoined the City to cease placement of all homeless families with children in the Catherine Street barracks-style family shelter in a former school building that contained hazardous lead paint and exposed asbestos and lacked adequate sanitary facilities. After renovations and an extensive evidentiary hearing, a 1987 trial court injunction permits use of the shelter for families subject to these conditions: 1) no families with children under the age of seven, no pregnant women, nor any child or adult who was mentally retarded could be placed in the shelter; 2) no family could be placed in the shelter for more than 30 days; 3) signs were to be posted in English and Spanish to advise women who might be pregnant of the danger to their unborn children of remaining in the shelter; and 4) the City was to adhere to an extensive 24-hour maintenance plan that it had devised to contain the danger of lead paint exposure for persons over the age of seven. Pursuant to a 1988 consent decree, the City agreed to remove all lead paint from the shelter and to convert the shelter from a barracks-style shelter to one with a private room for each family.

Gonzalez v. Martinique Hotel Affiliates, (Sup. Ct. N.Y. Co.) (Gammerman, J.):

• A 1985 trial court order prohibits a private hotel owner from implementing a "no-visitor" policy for homeless family residents. Claims in the litigation were based on State landlord-tenant law and constitutional rights of privacy and association.

Fulton v. Krauskopf, 117 A.D.2d 198 (1st Dep't 1986), modifying 127 Misc. 2d 20 (Sup. Ct. N.Y. Co. 1984):

• A 1986 Appellate Division decision affirms so much of a 1984 trial court order as required the City to provide homeless children and their parents with transportation grants to permit them to travel to school from distant emergency housing locations. As in Lamboy and Slade, claims were based on the "single State agency" provisions of State and federal law and State regulations requiring that principles enunciated in State administrative hearings be given "stare decisis" effect.

Jackson v. Grinker (S.D.N.Y.) (Leisure, J.):

• A 1989 consent order with the City and State provides for the implementation of "back-up" systems to ensure that eligible families and individuals receive their public assistance, food stamps, and Medicaid benefits in a timely fashion, even if errors resulting from the City's new Welfare Management System (WMS) computer prevents issuance of benefits under normal procedures. Thus, pursuant to the settlement, recipients whose benefits were delayed due to computer-related errors were entitled to receive their basic cash grant and Medicaid benefits on the day or the day after they were due, and their food stamp benefits within five days of their due date.

Cosentino v. Perales, 546 N.Y.S. 2d 75 (1st Dep't 1989), aff'g 524 N.Y.S. 2d 121 (Sup. Ct. N.Y. Co. 1987), State appeal denied, No. 1390, slip op. (Ct. of App. Jan. 9, 1990):

• A 1989 Appellate Division decision affirms a 1987 trial court order: 1) directing the City to develop individual case plans to provide child welfare preventive housing services to avert or abbreviate voluntary foster care placement; and 2) enjoining a State regulation limiting the provision of preventive services in the form of temporary housing to a period of 90 days. Settlement negotiations have been commenced regarding the City's failure to provide rent subsidies to prevent or shorten foster-care placement as required by new State statutory provisions.

In Re Chadbourne Industries Ltd/In Re Pan Trading Corp., (U.S. Bankruptcy Court, S.D.N.Y.) (Abram, J.):

- In 1987 and 1988, at the request of the Bankruptcy Court, representation is provided to tenant homeless families who had been placed at the Holland Hotel which was the subject of extensive bankruptcy court proceedings. Rulings in 1987 and 1988 deny applications by the debtor-in-possession and two subsequent trustees who had at various times sought to summarily remove homeless families from the premises and/or obtain rental payments on behalf of the families directly from the City in violation of State landlord-tenant law and a consent judgement in Montes v. Krauskopf involving public assistance rent restrictions. After an evidentiary hearing, a March 1988 order permits the City to purchase the hotel pursuant to a plan to provide all homeless families at the hotel with permanent housing and convert the building into a residence for homeless single adults.

In Re New York International Hostel, Inc., (U.S. Bankruptcy Court, S.D.N.Y.) (Brozman, J.):

- Representation is provided to homeless families placed at the Times Square Motor Inn, who intervened in this bankruptcy case involving the hotel in order to contest the appointment of a notorious welfare hotel owner to manage the hotel during the bankruptcy proceedings. After an extensive evidentiary hearing, a January 1989 order appoints an examiner to oversee the welfare hotel owner's daily operations. Based on the examiner's findings of mismanagement and enforcement efforts in McCain to enjoin placement of families at the hotel because of lead paint hazards at the hotel, the hotel owner resigned in January 1990, the City assumed direct operation of the hotel, and the homeless families were relocated to permanent housing by April 1990.

D & Z Holding Corp. v. The City of New York, (Sup. Ct. N.Y. Co.) (Freedman, J.):

- Representation is provided to homeless family residents of the Bayview Hotel who intervened in litigation by the hotel owners challenging the

D & Z Holding Corp. v. The City of New York, continued

City's determination to cease placing families in the hotel pursuant to the 1990 McCain consent order. A May 1990 Kings County trial court order transfers the venue from Kings County to New York County where the case can be heard along with the McCain proceedings, and the Appellate Division, Second Department, declines to reverse the venue order. The trial court in New York County grants intervention and denies the hotel owners a temporary restraining order to require the City to continue to place families at the hotel. A July 1990 consent order provides for dismissal of the case.

Hamilton Place Associates v. City of New York, (S.D.N.Y.) (Kram, J.):

• Representation is provided to homeless families who moved to intervene in anti-trust litigation commenced by the owners of the Hamilton Hotel, who were challenging the City's determination to cease placing homeless families at the hotel pursuant to the 1990 McCain consent order. An October 1990 consent order provides for dismissal of the case.

O'Donovan v. Dinkins, N.Y.L.J., Jan. 29, 1993, at 25, col. 1 (Sup. Ct. Richmond Co.) (Amann, J.):

• Representation is provided to homeless family residents of the Angels by the Sea Family Shelter in Staten Island who intervene in a proceeding commenced by local elected officials and community residents to enjoin use of the facility based on claims that the City had failed to comply with land-use procedures in determining to place families in the not-for-profit shelter. A November 1992 trial court order grants intervention, and a January 1993 decision denies the request by the elected officials and community residents for an injunction prohibiting use of the facility.

Special thanks to Helaine Barnett at Legal Aid for her preparation of this section, and for her dedication to helping homeless families.

APPENDIX III

RET Center Funding Mechanisms

While the RET center model presents a convincing argument regarding its effectiveness, the more difficult debate concerns its affordability. Seemingly expensive, RET centers are in fact more economical than less program-rich emergency shelters or welfare hotels. The overall cost of operating RET centers, emergency shelters, and welfare hotels are about the same. *However*, dollar for dollar RET centers dedicate at least six times more to programs and services than emergency shelters and welfare hotels.

The financing mechanism for the RET center model is a creative and interlocking series of public and private grants. For the most part the operation, or the debt service and residential, child care and social services costs of the centers are funded through the Emergency Assistance (EA) funding stream of Aid to Families with Dependent Children.[1] The EA funding stream enables localities to leverage 25 and 50 percent of the overall funding from the state and federal governments respectively for the shelter services rendered. In other words, at an average cost of $100 per day, localities pay only $25 in local tax levy for each family housed in a RET center. With an average of three members in each family, the cost to localities for the entire RET center operation is $8.33 per person per day.

Moreover, RET centers offer an attractive potential for other government and private funders whose funding builds on an existing economy of scale. Traditional funding bottlenecks such as administrative overhead, and lease or capital costs are non-issues as the physical infrastructure is already funded. Thus, while the actual program costs are purely incremental, the value of a program far exceeds the actual investment: the physical space is a given, the program beneficiaries live on-site, and all programs mutually reinforce the same overall goals. In sum, RET centers offer an opportunity to recycle government dollars several times and stretch foundation, corporate, and other government funding much further.

The potential for replicating the RET center model nationwide has never been greater. The federal Resolution Trust Company currently holds tens of thousands of residential properties in move-in condition. Thus by removing the element of capital financing, government has the potential to significantly reduce to RET center operating costs and save hundreds of millions of dollars. In addition by equipping families to face the challenges of independent living, RET centers also hold the potential to reduce the welfare rolls by millions of dollars through helping homeless heads of households become more capable as tenants, consumers, employees, community leaders, and most importantly parents. The financial return on instituting the RET center model holds great promise for government, taxpayers, and homeless families alike.

[1] Established in 1967, Emergency Assistance allows states to provide funding for up to a 30-day period for services to families in order to avoid the destitution of children. In the mid 1980s the provision of this funding was extended to cover the shelter costs for homeless families with a moratorium placed on the 30 day limit.

NOTES

CHAPTER 1

1. Children's Defense Fund, *Leave No Child Behind: An Opinion Maker's Guide to Children in Election Year 1992* (Washington, DC: Children's Defense Fund), 1991, p. 28.

2. Since 1986, the annual surveys conducted by the U.S. Conference of Mayors—generally considered among the most complete of homeless surveys—have estimated that families with children make up one-third of the national homeless population. Other studies have put this figure between 26 and 36 percent. By comparison, in 1980, homeless families made up only 10 percent of the nation's homeless. Cities with particularly high percentages of homeless children include Portland, Oregon; Trenton, New Jersey; and Norfolk, Virginia. In New York City, children comprise 36 percent of the homeless population in city shelters, representing the city's largest homeless subgroup. In Rhode Island in 1990, half of those seeking shelters were

families. Children accounted for 27 percent of the state's homeless that year. U.S. Conference of Mayors, *A Status Report on Homeless Families in America's Cities: A 29-City Survey* (Washington, DC: U.S. Conference of Mayors), May 1987; L.M. Reyes and L.D. Waxman, *A Status Report on Hunger and Homelessness in America's Cities, 1989: A 27-City Survey* (Washington, DC: U.S. Conference of Mayors), 1989; J. Parvensky and D. Krasniewski, *In Search of a Place to Call Home: A Profile of Homelessness in Colorado* (Denver, CO: Colorado Coalition for the Homeless), 1988; S. Peuquet and P. Leland, *Homelessness in Delaware* (Neward, DE: University of Delaware), 1988; Y.M. Vissing, "Homeless Children Having Children," *New England Journal of Public Policy* 8 (Spring-Summer 1992), p. 394; New York City Commission on the Homeless, *The Way Home: A New Direction in Social Policy* (New York: Commission on the Homeless), 1992; J. Tull, "Homelessness: An Overview," *New England Journal of Public Policy* 8 (Spring-Summer 1992).

Mihaly derived the estimate of 2.0 million homeless children nationwide from estimates of homeless children in California. She notes that if the same proportion of children were homeless nationally as were homeless in that state in 1989 (159,000 to 200,000), there were between 1.6 and 2.0 million children homeless across the country that year.

L.K. Mihaly, *Homeless Families: Failed Policies and Young Victims* (Washington, DC: Children's Defense Fund), January 1991.

3. Among homeless families with children, approximately 80 percent are headed by single women. M.R. Burt, *Over the Edge: The Growth of Homelessness in the 1980s* (New York: Russell Sage Foundation), 1992, p. 62.

Significant geographic differences do exist, however. In the American Southwest, for example, 70 percent of homeless families are headed by women, compared to 85 percent in the Northeast. E.L. Bassuk, R.W. Carman and L.F. Weinreb, eds., *Community Care for Homeless Families: A Program Design Manual* (Newton Centre, MA: The Better Homes Foundation), 1990, p. 7.

See also C. Mills and H. Ota, "Homeless Women with Minor Children in the Detroit Metropolitan Area," *Social Work* 34 (1989), pp. 485-489; P.W. Dail, "The Psychosocial Context of Homeless Mothers with Young Children:

Program and Policy Implications," *Child Welfare* 69 (July-August 1990), pp. 291-308; New York City Commission on the Homeless, *The Way Home*, p. B-3.

At HFH, fewer than one in 10 mothers receive some form of child support from their children's fathers. Regarding educational levels, although no national data are available, a 1991 New York City study found that nearly half (45 percent) of homeless parents residing in family shelters had less than a high school education. A 1989 study found even higher rates: 60 percent of homeless parents in New York City had not graduated from high school (51 percent had 8 to 11 years of schooling and 9 percent had an eighth grade education or less). This study also found that only 33 percent of the parents had at least one year of full-time work experience. Among those age 25 and under, only 25 percent had such work experience. A study conducted in California also found that homeless parents had less education and were less likely to have held a full-time job than "unattached" homeless individuals.

New York City Commission on the Homeless, *The Way Home*, p. 65; J.R. Knickman and B.C. Weitzman, *A Study of Homeless Families in New York City: Risk Assessment Models and Strategies for Prevention (Final Report, Volume 1)* (New York: Health Research Program of New York University), 1989, p. 65; The Stanford Center for the Study of Families, Children and Youth, *The Stanford Study of Homeless Families, Children and Youth* (Palo Alto, CA: Stanford Center for the Study of Families, Children and Youth), November 1991, p. 10.

See also Mills and Ota, "Homeless Women with Minor Children in the Detroit Metropolitan Area," pp. 485-489.

A 1988 study in Boston revealed that 40 percent of female heads of homeless families had been abused, compared to 20 percent of poor housed mothers. Findings from several studies conducted in 1990 New York and Los Angeles concur with this information. See P.J. Fischer, "Victimization and Homelessness," *New England Journal of Public Policy* 8 (Spring-Summer 1992), p. 233.

See also Mills and Ota, "Homeless Women With Minor Children In The Detroit Metropolitan Area;" E.L. Bassuk, L. Rubin and A.S. Lauriat, "Characteristics of Sheltered Homeless Families," *American Journal of Public Health* 76 (September 1986), pp. 1097-1101; Dail, "Psychosocial

Context of Homeless Mothers;" Knickman and Weitzman, *A Study of Homeless Families in New York City*.

Regarding the lack of community and family support structures for homeless families, see Stanford Center for the Study of Families, Children and Youth, *The Stanford Study of Homeless Families, Children and Youth*, pp. 15-16; K.Y. McChesney, "New Findings on Homeless Families," *Family Professional* 1 (1986); E.L. Bassuk and L. Rosenberg, "Why Does Family Homelessness Occur? A Case-Control Study," *American Journal of Public Health* 78 (July 1988); R. Wallace and E.L. Bassuk, "Housing Famine and Homelessness: How the Low-Income Housing Crisis Affects Families with Inadequate Supports," *Environment and Planning* 23 (1991).

4. Over half (3.1 million) of the nation's 5.3 million poor children live in families headed by single mothers (2.1 million, or 40 percent, live in families headed by married couples). Of these single mothers, nearly 40 percent have no more than an 8th grade education. For women of color, the situation is even worse: 60 percent of families headed by single African-American women are poor, as are 51 percent of families headed by single Latinas. In 1989, the median income for households supported by African-American single mothers was $9,710, or $5,647 below the poverty line. National Center for Children in Poverty, *Five Million Children: 1992 Update* (New York: Columbia University School of Public Health), 1992, p. 5; U.S. Census data cited in K.Y. McChesney, "Macroeconomic Issues in Poverty: Implication for Child and Youth Homelessness," in J.H. Kryder-Coe, L.M. Salamon and J.M. Molnar, eds., *Homeless Children and Youth: A New American Dilemma* (New Brunswick, NJ: Transaction Publishers), 1991, p. 145.

For information about education, work histories, and social supports for both housed and homeless single women, see Bassuk and Rosenberg, "Why Does Family Homelessness Occur?"

According to the Children's Defense Fund, a typical poor family with children in the U.S. spends 70 percent of its income on housing. They spend another 25 percent for child care, according to the National Research Council. Children's Defense Fund, *Leave No Child Behind*, p. 56.

For more on other challenges faced by American families today, see

I. Garfinkel and S.S. McLanahan, *Single Mothers And Their Children: A New American Dilemma* (Washington, DC: The Urban Institute Press), 1986; S.A. Hewlett, *When The Bough Breaks: The Cost Of Neglecting Our Children* (New York: Basic Books), 1991; C.M. Johnson, A.M. Sum and J.D. Weill, *Vanishing Dreams: The Growing Economic Plight Of America's Young Families* (Washington, DC: Children's Defense Fund), 1988.

Regarding the history of government assistance to families, in 1979, government assistance prevented one in five families from crossing the poverty line; by 1991, only one in eight. Children's Defense Fund, *State of America's Children 1992* (Washington, DC: Children's Defense Fund), 1992, p. 27. See also D.T. Ellwood, *Poor Support: Poverty in the American Family* (New York: Basic Books), 1988.

5. For more on Great Depression and post-WWII (1950s and 1960s) homelessness, see Burt, *Over the Edge*; L. Blumberg, T. Shipley, Jr. and I.W. Shandler, *Skid Row and Its Alternatives* (Philadelphia, PA: Temple University Press), 1973; D.B. Bogue, *Skid Row in American Cities* (Chicago: Community and Family Study Center, University of Chicago), 1963; J.M. Crouse, *The Homeless Transient in the Great Depression: New York State, 1929-1941* (Albany, NY: SUNY Press), 1986; D. Shaw, C. Roberts, B. Swaze and P. Nelson, *Homelessness: A Blight on the American Landscape* (New York: Sage Publishers), 1990; P.H. Rossi, *The Family, Welfare and Homelessness* (Chicago: University of Chicago Press), 1989; P.H. Rossi, "The Old Homeless And New Homeless In Historical Perspective," *American Psychologist* 45 (August 1990).

6. R.K. Schutt and G.R. Garrett, *Responding to the Homeless: Policy and Practice* (New York: Plenum Press), 1992, pp. 6-9. See also P.H. Rossi, *Down and Out in America: The Origins of Homelessness* (Chicago: University of Chicago Press), 1989.

On the issue of deinstitutionalization and homelessness, in 1955 there were 552,150 mentally ill people in institutions; by 1980, that figure had dropped 80 percent to 118,743. See E.F. Torrey, *Nowhere to Go* (New York: Harper & Row Publishers), 1988; M. Hope and J. Young, "From Back Wards to Back Alleys: Deinstitutionalization and the Homeless," *Urban and Social*

Change Review 17 (1984); M. Greenblatt, "Deinstitutionalization and Reinstitutionalization of the Mentally Ill," in M.J. Robertson and M. Greenblatt, eds., *Homelessness: A National Perspective* (New York: Plenum Press), 1992.

Other factors, however, also played major roles in this period's homelessness increases, including decriminalization of public drunkenness, more rigid commitment laws, and changes in the administration of public welfare. See Schutt and Garrett, *Responding to the Homeless*; K. Hopper and J. Hamberg, *The Making of America's Homeless: From Skid Row to New Poor 1945-1984* (New York: Community Service Society), 1984.

For information on housing policy and the loss of SROs and low-income housing, see R.D. Kerr, "Shelter the American Way: Federal Urban Housing Policy, 1900-1980," *New England Journal of Public Policy* 8 (Spring-Summer 1992); Schutt and Garrett, *Responding to the Homeless*.

7. J. Molnar, *Home is Where the Heart Is: The Crisis of Homeless Children and Families in New York City* (New York: Bank Street College of Education), 1988, pp. 10-11; Joint Center for Housing Studies, *The State of the Nation's Housing 1990* (Washington, DC: Joint Center for Housing Studies), 1990.

On housing availability in the 1980s, including increasing problems for women and housing, see Rutgers Center for Urban Policy Research, *The Unsheltered Woman: Women and Housing in the '80s* (New Brunswick, NJ: Rutgers Center for Urban Policy Research), 1985. See also J. Leavitt, "Homelessness and the Housing Crisis," in M.J. Robertson and M. Greenblatt, eds., *Homelessness: A National Perspective* (New York: Plenum Press), 1992; Knickman and Weitzman, *A Study of Homeless Families in New York City*; National Alliance to End Homelessness, *Housing and Homelessness* (Washington, DC: National Alliance to End Homelessness), 1988; M.A. Stegman, "Remedies for Homelessness: An Analysis of Potential Housing Policy and Program Responses," in J.H. Kryder-Coe, L.M. Salamon and J.M. Molnar, *Homeless Children and Youth: A New American Dilemma* (New Brunswick, NJ: Transaction Publishers), 1991, pp. 228-231.

Regarding the role of business cycles and unemployment, according to the Bureau of Labor Statistics, an estimated 2.2 million people were dislocated from their jobs because of layoffs or business closures every year between

January 1981 and January 1986. In addition, between 1980 and 1988, the minimum wage value decreased 31 percent. National Coalition for the Homeless, *Homelessness in the United States: Background and Federal Response, A Briefing Paper for Presidential Candidates* (Washington, DC: National Coalition for the Homeless), 1987; K.Y. McChesney, "Macroeconomic Issues in Poverty: Implications for Child and Youth Homelessness," in J.H. Kryder-Coe, L.M. Salamon and J.M. Molnar, eds., *Homeless Children and Youth: A New American Dilemma* (New Brunswick, NJ: Transaction Publishers), 1991; J.D. Kasarda, "Jobs, Migration, And Emerging Urban Mismatches," in M.G.H. McGeary and L.E. Lynn, Jr., eds., *Urban Change and Poverty* (Washington, DC: National Academy Press), 1988.

Concerning income levels for female-headed families, see U.S. House of Representatives, Committee on Ways and Means, *Overview of Entitlement Programs: The 1990 Green Book* (Washington, DC: U.S. Government Printing Office), 1990; figures cited in E.S. Merves, "Homeless Women: Beyond the Bag Lady Myth," in M.J. Robertson and M. Greenblatt, eds., *Homelessness: A National Perspective* (New York: Plenum Press), 1992.

8. Between 1970 and 1981, an average of 72 percent of all American poor children received AFDC. Between the time the Omnibus Budget Reconciliation Act (OBRA) took effect in 1982 and the end of 1987, only an average of 54 percent of poor children received such assistance. Between 1981 and 1989, Food Stamp benefits dropped 13 percent (in real terms). Between 1978 and 1987, overall federal funding (in constant dollars) of child-oriented programs, including AFDC, Head Start, Food Stamps, and those related to child nutrition and child health, shrank by over 4 percent. See figures cited in Burt, *Over the Edge*, pp. 83-87; R.B. Reich, "As the World Turns," *New Republic* 3876 (1989), p. 28; Mihaly, *Homeless Families*, p. 14; Hewlett, *When the Bough Breaks*, pp. 45, 148.

See also Garfinkel and McLanahan, *Single Mothers And Their Children;* Ellwood, *Poor Support.* For more on 1980s federal social policy, see J.L. Palmer and I.F. Sawhill, eds., *The Reagan Record* (Cambridge, MA: Ballinger Publishing Co.), 1984.

9. R.B. Reich, "What is a Nation?," *Political Science Quarterly* 106 (1991), pp. 193-209.

In more than half of the states, school funding systems that are based on property taxes have been sued by poorer districts who charge that such systems create unequal educational opportunities. Missouri has already declared that the state education financing system violates the constitutional right to education. In Illinois, per capita spending for students attending schools in suburban Chicago's New Trier district is $10,417, but in much poorer East St. Louis it is only half that amount. The results are clearly different: New Trier High School is equipped with computer labs, offers a wide range of courses, including 18 college-level classes, and has class sizes of 20 pupils or less. In East St. Louis, no college-level courses are available and a typical high school class averages more than 30 students. Where textbooks can be replaced yearly at New Trier, the average wait is five to 10 years in East St. Louis. In Missouri, per capita spending on students in the state's richest districts averages $9,750 versus $2,653 in the poorest districts.

J. Zuckman, "The Next Education Crisis: Equalizing School Funds," *Congressional Quarterly Weekly Report* 51 (March 27, 1993), pp. 749-754; M. Jordan, "Issues That Won't Go Away," *America's Agenda* (Spring 1993), p. 8; J.M. Simmons, B. Finlay and A. Yang, *The Adolescent and Young Adult Fact Book* (Washington, DC: Children's Defense Fund), 1991; National Commission on Children, *Beyond Rhetoric: A New American Agenda for Children and Families* (Washington, DC: U.S. Government Printing Office), 1991. For an especially poignant account of the disparities separating public schools across the country, see J. Kozol, *Savage Inequalities: Children in America's Schools* (New York: Harper Perennial), 1991.

10. By 1989, funding for the federal family planning program was only half what it had been in 1981. Even by 1984, overall federal expenditures for social services had dropped by 25 percent.

Between 1980 and 1991 the number of children reported abused or neglected tripled, and from 1985 to 1991 that number rose by 40 percent. Between 1970 and 1988 births to unmarried teenagers surged 64 percent, and between 1980 and 1988 alone such births increased 33 percent. In 1990, teenage pregnancy in the U.S. was at its highest level since 1972 (at 59.9 births per 1000 females aged 15-19). Nearly 70 percent of these births were to unmarried teens, the highest proportion ever recorded in the U.S. and a 588 percent increase from 1960, when the proportion stood at 11.5 percent. And between 1984 and 1988, drug abuse admissions to treatment programs more than doubled (from 253,400 to 518,900) and the number of emergency room cases involving cocaine rose 311 percent.

See Ellwood, *Poor Support*, p. 32; Hewlett, *When the Bough Breaks;* Children's Defense Fund, *The State of America's Children*; Simmons, et al.; *The Adolescent and Young Adult Fact Book*, p. 136; Children's Defense Fund, "Births to Teens," *CDF Reports* 14, No. 7 (June 1993), pp. 7-8; U.S. Advisory Board on Child Abuse and Neglect, *Child Abuse and Neglect: Critical First Steps in Response to a National Emergency* (Washington, DC: U.S. Department of Health and Human Services), August 1990; Burt, *Over the Edge*, p. 114.

11. According to relatively conservative estimates, there were between 250,000 to 300,000 homeless Americans in 1983 and 500,000 to 700,000 in 1987. U.S. Department of Housing and Urban Development, Office of Policy Development and Research, *A Report to the Secretary on the Homeless and Emergency Shelters* (Washington, DC: Department of Housing and Urban Development), 1984; M.R. Burt and B.E. Cohen, *America's Homeless: Numbers, Characteristics, and the Programs that Serve Them* (Washington, DC: The Urban Institute), 1991, p. 25; Interagency Council on the Homeless, "How Many Homeless People Are There?," *Fact Sheet* (April 1991).

For more on the pre-McKinney federal response to homelessness, see J. Blau, *The Visible Poor: Homelessness in the United States* (New York: Oxford University Press), 1992; R. Wasem, *Homelessness: Issues and Legislation in 1988* (Washington, DC: Congressional Research Service), 1988.

See also Stewart B. McKinney Homelessness Assistance Act, Public Law 100-77 (July 2, 1987), codified as 42 U.S.C. SS11301-11472.

12. In its first year (FY 1987), $355 million was allocated for McKinney programs. By FY 1991, that initial outlay had nearly doubled to $680 million. A year later, the amount increased another 30 percent to $882 million. For FY 1993, Congress appropriated $945.9 million, a tripling of the McKinney budget in only six years. The budget request for 1993 also included $119

million for targeted non-McKinney homeless assistance. Overall, McKinney expenditures totaled only 0.05 percent of government spending in 1991 compared to the 0.2 percent or the 0.4 percent of the total population the homeless comprise (based on estimates of 500,000 and 1,000,000 homeless people respectively). Interagency Council on the Homeless, "How Much is the Federal Government Spending on Programs to Help the Homeless?," *Fact Sheet* (April 1992); National Coalition for the Homeless, *The Closing Door: Economic Causes of Homelessness* (Washington, DC: National Coalition for the Homeless), 1990, p. 2.

"The McKinney Act provides primarily emergency relief addressing the immediate survival needs of homeless persons." National Law Center on Homelessness and Poverty, *Beyond McKinney: Policies to End Homelessness* (Washington, DC: National Law Center on Homelessness and Poverty), November 1992, p. 1; The Interagency Council on the Homeless, *The McKinney Act: A Program Guide* (Washington, DC: Interagency Council on the Homeless), January 1992; Mihaly, *Homeless Families*, p. 17.

In FY 1993, the Education for Homeless Children and Youth Program garnered only $24.8 million in appropriations, and the Job Training for the Homeless program, $12.54 million. In contrast, $50 million went to emergency shelters and $105 million to the SRO Mod Rehab program. National Alliance to End Homelessness, "Budget Figures for Fiscal Year 1994," *Alliance* 9 (May 1993), p. 5.

In 1991, when the McKinney Act was reauthorized, Congress included provisions to provide comprehensive services to previously homeless families and families at risk of becoming homeless but did not appropriate money accordingly. By FY 1992, only $48.2 million was appropriated for prevention programs, primarily in the form of increased Food Stamp benefits. In FY 1994, President Clinton has requested $107.8 million to the SRO Mod Rehab program, but only a minimal increase in funding for the Education for Homeless Children and Youth program, to $25.5 million (up from $24 million in FY 1993). At the same time, however, Clinton has become the first president to request funding for the Family Reunification Program, asking for $77 million. The President has also requested a huge increase in spending for supportive housing, asking for $350 million versus the $150 million 1993 appropriation. A.L. Solarz, "To Be Young and Homeless: The Implications of Homelessness for Children," in M.J. Robertson and M. Greenblatt, eds., *Homelessness: A National Perspective* (New York: Plenum Press), 1992, p. 284; Interagency Council on the Homeless, *Federal Progress Toward Ending Homelessness* (Washington, DC: Interagency Council on the Homeless), September 1992, p. 34; National Alliance to End Homelessness, "Budget Figures for Fiscal Year 1994," p. 5.

13. For example, funding for facilities comes from one source, money for operating costs comes from another, and money for staff from yet a third. Moreover, a state cannot be certain that necessary funding for all portions of its plan will be accessible. In addition, in one survey, states complained that application deadlines were too close together for already understaffed state agencies to submit all the necessary proposals to the appropriate departments. M.R. Burt and B. Cohen, *State Activities and Programs for the Homeless: A Review of Six States* (Washington, DC: The Urban Institute), 1988, p. 118; Blau, *The Visible Poor*, pp. 111-116. See also National Alliance to End Homelessness, "National Groups Brief Congressional Staff on Solutions to Homelessness," *Alliance* 9 (May 1993), p. 5.

14. R.I. Jahiel, "Health and Health Care of Homeless People," in M.J. Robertson and M. Greenblatt, eds., *Homelessness: A National Perspective* (New York: Plenum Press), 1992, p. 154. Congress appropriated only $335 million of the $432 million authorized for fiscal year 1987 and only $364 million of the $616 million authorized for 1988. Blau, *The Visible Poor*, pp. 111-116.

See also U.S. Conference of Mayors, *Status Report on the Stewart B. McKinney Homeless Assistance Act of 1987* (Washington, DC: U.S. Conference of Mayors), June 1988; L. Walker, "HUD's Administration of the McKinney Act: A Problem of State-Federal Relations," *The Journal of State Government* 63 (January-March 1990).

Federal Emergency Assistance programs continue to operate without any mechanism for monitoring and controlling the quality of services homeless families receive—or do not receive. Molnar, *Home is Where the Heart Is*, p. 94; Blau, *The Visible Poor,* pp. 113-114; U.S. General Accounting Office,

Homelessness: Access to McKinney Act Programs Improved But Better Oversight Needed GAO/RCED-91-29 (Washington, DC: U.S. General Accounting Office), December 1990; U.S. General Accounting Office, *Homelessness: Transitional Housing Shows Initial Success But Long-Term Effects Unknown* (GAO/RCED-91-200), September 1991.

15. A 1990 survey of 30 American cities found that nearly half (41 percent) of homeless spending was locally generated and 35 percent came from state funds. Only 23 percent came from the federal government. U.S. Conference of Mayors, *A Status Report On Hunger And Homelessness in America's Cities* (1990), pp. 46-47. See also Blau, *The Visible Poor*, pp. 109-132.

Regarding the crisis orientation of governmental institutions designed to aid the homeless, see E.L. Bassuk, "The Problem of Family Homelessness," in E.L. Bassuk, R.W. Caman and L.F. Weinreb, eds., *Community Care for Homeless Families: A Program Design Manual* (Newton Centre, MA: The Better Homes Foundation), 1990, pp. 10-11; N.K. Kaufman, "State Government's Response to Homelessness: The Massachusetts Experience, 1983-1990," *New England Journal of Public Policy* 8 (Spring-Summer 1992), p. 481.

Even private funders have focused on emergency responses: a survey of such funders in Massachusetts found that 80 percent spent the majority of their funds on emergency services, although funding to transitional housing programs has increased over the past several years. N. Robb and R. McCambridge, "Private Funders: Their Role in Homelessness Projects," *New England Journal of Public Policy* 8 (Spring-Summer 1992).

16. Burt and Cohen, *State Activities and Programs for the Homeless*, p. 3; Burt and Cohen, *America's Homeless*, pp. 141-142.

17. State constitutions also have stood as barriers to needed programs. Many constitutions contain provisions that deny the appropriation of funds to religious organizations (which often play a vital role in combating homelessness in the private sector) or restrict the carry-over of funds from year to year. Burt and Cohen, *State Activities and Programs for the Homeless*, p. 119.

Even governors acknowledge the inadequacy of the governmental response: in a 1988 survey of governors, 89 percent said the federal government was doing an inadequate job responding to homelessness, and 81 percent acknowledged that their own response fell short. The Better Homes Foundation, *Final Report: Evaluation of Programs for Homeless Families* (Newton Centre, MA: Better Homes Foundation), 1990; L. Walker, *Homelessness in the States* (Lexington, KY: Council of State Governments), 1989; Burt and Cohen, *America's Homeless.*

18. D.W. Kirchheimer, "Sheltering the Homeless in New York City: Expansion in an Era of Government Expansion," *Political Science Quarterly* 104 (1989-1990); New York City Human Resources Administration, Adult Services Administration, Bureau of Management Information Systems, *Update to the Single and Family Shelter Statistics* (New York: New York City Human Resources Administration), March 1991.

19. New York City Human Resources Administration, Adult Services Administration, Bureau of Management Information Systems, *Update to the Single and Family Shelter Statistics.*

20. New York City Human Resources Administration, Adult Services Administration, Bureau of Management Information Systems, *Emergency Housing Services for Homeless Families: Monthly Report* (New York: New York City Human Resources Administration), May 1993. New York City Office of the Mayor, David N. Dinkins, *Revised and Updated Plan for Housing and Assisting Homeless Single Adults and Families* (New York: New York City Mayor's Office on Homelessness and SRO Housing), March 1993, p. 44.

21. See Appendix I for description of HFH's statistical methodology.

22. In 1984, the infant mortality rate for infants born to homeless mothers residing at welfare hotels was 24.9 per thousand, compared to 12.0 for all others in New York City. Molnar, however, believes that by 1987 the IMR

among homeless mothers had likely increased to greater than 27.6 per thousand. Molnar, *Home is Where the Heart Is*, p. 40. See also W. Chavkin, A. Kristal, C. Seabron and P.E. Guigli, "Reproductive Experience of Women Living in Hotels for the Homeless in New York City," *New York State Journal of Medicine* 87 (1987), pp. 10-13. See Chapter 5 for more in-depth discussion of homeless children's health problems.

23. Funding for homeless families began in 1982. In a 1988 federal survey of the nation's largest cities, at $757 million New York City spent 16 times more in local funds on the homeless problem than the next highest-spending city, Philadelphia. For detailed analyses of the evolution of New York City policy between 1978 and 1985 and the forces involved in shaping it, see Kirchheimer, "Sheltering the Homeless in New York City;" Blau, *The Visible Poor*, pp. 133-169. See also U.S. Department of Housing and Urban Development, *Homeless Assistance Policy and Practice in the Nation's Five Largest Cities* (Washington, DC: U.S. Department of Housing and Urban Development), 1989.

Regarding the city's expenditure of $400 million, it should be noted that this figure does not include the hundreds of millions more spent by the city and state on capital improvements related to homelessness. See New York City Commission on the Homeless, *The Way Home*, p. 3.

24. Blau, *The Visible Poor*, pp. 109-169. For a recent presentation of the city's views of the system and the need for change, see New York City Office of the Mayor, David N. Dinkins, *Revised and Updated Plan for Housing and Assisting Homeless Single Adults and Families*. See also New York City Commission on the Homeless, *The Way Home*; Molnar, *Home is Where the Heart Is*.

25. Molnar, *Home is Where the Heart Is*, pp. 25-29. For further discussion of the conditions and costs associated with the hotels, see J. Kozol, *Rachel and Her Children* (New York: Crown Publishers), 1988; J.H. Simpson, M. Kilduff and C.D. Blewett, *Struggling to Survive in a Welfare Hotel* (New York: Community Service Society), 1984.

26. By continuing to use Tier I's and hotels, the city remains in violation of city law enacted in mid-1990, as well as state regulations and court orders. The city is also at risk of losing federal funds. Citizens' Committee for Children, *On Their Own—At What Cost? A Look at Families Who Leave Shelters* (New York: Citizens' Committee for Children), May 1992, p. 9.

27. Molnar, *Home is Where the Heart Is*, pp. 97-98.

28. New York City Office of the Mayor, David N. Dinkins, *Revised and Updated Plan for Housing and Assisting Homeless Single Adults and Families*, p. 7.

CHAPTER 2

1. Citizens' Committee for Children, *On Their Own—At What Cost?*, p. 19; New York City Commission on the Homeless, *The Way Home*, p. 75.

2. New York City Office of the Mayor, David N. Dinkins, *Revised and Updated Plan for Housing and Assisting Homeless Single Adults and Families*, pp. 47-48. See also A.L. Solarz, "To Be Young and Homeless," in M.J. Robertson and M. Greenblatt, eds., *Homelessness: A National Perspective* (New York: Plenum Press) 1992, pp. 275-286; Molnar, *Home is Where the Heart Is*.

Long waits are not unique to New York City; one survey of the California shelter system found that the average wait for Section 8 housing in the Bay Area was two years. See Stanford Center for the Study of Families, Children and Youth, *The Stanford Study of Homeless Families, Children and Youth*.

3. In Schutt and Garrett's words, "Homelessness is a manifestation of a larger complex of interrelated social problems. Homelessness will decline in tandem with reductions in drug abuse, child abuse and neglect, and alcoholism; and with improvements in education, familial and community-based social supports, jobs and health care." Schutt and Garrett, eds., *Responding to the Homeless*, p. 220.

See also Burt, *Over the Edge*; A.S. Lauriat, "Sheltering Homeless Families: Beyond An Emergency Response," in E.L. Bassuk, ed., *The Mental Health Needs of Homeless Persons* (San Francisco: Jossey-Bass), 1986, pp. 87-94; Molnar, *Home is Where the Heart Is*, p. 93; C. Friedmutter, "Service-Enriched Housing for Homeless Families," unpublished report prepared for the Robert Wood Johnson Foundation (Princeton, NJ), February 1989; M. Argeriou, "Homelessness in Massachusetts: Perception, Policy, and Progress," *New England Journal of Public Policy* 8 (Spring-Summer 1992).

Regarding increasing support for integrated centers, Schutt and Garrett conclude that case management combined with a residential program is "very effective," although their examples of such a model apply specifically to the mentally ill and alcoholics. Schutt and Garrett, *Responding to the Homelessness*, pp. 43-44, p. 220.

See also Lauriat, "Sheltering Homeless Families," p. 93; M.R. Stoner, "The Plight of the Homeless Woman," in J. Erickson and C. Wilhelm, eds., *Housing the Homeless* (New York: Center for Urban Policy Research), 1984; Molnar, *Home is Where the Heart Is*, pp. 93-105; Friedmutter, "Service-Enriched Housing for Homeless Families."

4. New York City Commission on the Homeless, *The Way Home*, p. 75.

CHAPTER 3

1. For recent reviews of research findings on the effects of homelessness on children, see J.M. Molnar, W.R. Rath and T.P. Klein, "Constantly Compromised: The Impact of Homelessness on Children," *Journal of Social Issues* 46 (1990); Y. Rafferty and M. Shinn, "The Impact of Homelessness on Children," *American Psychologist* 46 (1991); T. Klein, C. Bittel and J. Molnar, *No Place to Call Home: Supporting the Needs of Homeless Children in the Early Childhood Classroom* (New York: All Children's House), 1992; J. Martin, "The Trauma of Homelessness," *International Journal of Mental Health* 20 (1991).

The National Coalition for the Homeless estimates that 57 percent of homeless children miss school altogether. Another study from 1988, of families seeking aid from the Traveler's Aid Society, found 43 percent of these children were not attending school. National Coalition for the Homeless, *Broken Lives: Denial of Education to Homeless Children* (Washington, DC: National Coalition for the Homeless), 1987; P.L. Maza and J.A. Hall, *Homeless Children and Their Families: A Preliminary Study* (Washington, DC: Child Welfare League of America), 1988; U.S. Dept. of Education, *Report to Congress: State Interim Report on the Education of Homeless Children* (Washington, DC: U.S. Department of Education), February 1985; Y. Rafferty, "Developmental and Educational Consequences of Homelessness on Children and Youth," in J.H. Kryder-Coe, L.M. Salamon and J.M. Molnar, eds., *Homeless Children and Youth: A New American Dilemma* (New Brunswick, NJ: Transaction Publishers), 1991.

On the impact of homelessness for truancy rates, see Rafferty, "Developmental and Educational Consequences of Homelessness on Children and Youth;" D.L. Wood, R.B. Valdez, T. Hayashi and A. Shen, "Health of Homeless Children and Housed, Poor Children," *Pediatrics* 86 (1990); U.S. Department of Education, *Report to Congress*; Y. Rafferty and N. Rollins, *Learning in Limbo: The Educational Deprivation of Homeless Children* (New York: Advocates for Children), 1989; Bassuk, Rubin and Lauriat, "Characteristics of Sheltered Homeless Families;" E. Bassuk and L. Rubin, "Homeless Children: A Neglected Population," *American Journal of Orthopsychiatry* 57 (1987).

Regarding the consequences of homelessness for educational achievement, see Rafferty and Rollins, *Learning in Limbo*; Wood, et al., "Health of Homeless Children and Housed, Poor Children;" Bassuk and Rubin, "Homeless Children;" E.L. Bassuk and L. Rosenberg, "Psychosocial Characteristics of Homeless Children and Children With Homes," *Pediatrics* 85 (1990); Maza and Hall, *Homeless Children and Their Families*; D. Wood, T. Hayashi, K. Schlossman and R.B. Valdez, *Over the Brink: Homeless Families in Los Angeles* (Sacramento, CA: California Assembly Office of Research), 1989.

2. Based on Board of Education data, Rafferty found that homeless children had a 74 percent attendance rate in elementary school (versus 89 percent citywide), 64 percent in junior high (versus 86 percent citywide) and only 51 percent in high school (versus 84 percent citywide). Only 28 percent of homeless students "scored at or above grade level" in math (versus 57 percent

citywide) and only 42 percent in reading (versus 68 percent citywide). Rafferty, "Developmental and Educational Consequences of Homelessness on Children and Youth." See also Rafferty and Rollins, *Learning in Limbo.*

3. Twenty percent of school-aged children living in Homes for the Homeless facilities have been placed in special education classes due to developmental delays, and 37 percent have repeated a grade. Only 23 percent of homeless children score at grade level in math and 38 percent score at grade level in reading. Institute for Children and Poverty, "Access to Success: Meeting the Educational Needs of Homeless Children and Families," *Homes For the Homeless Quarterly Reports* 1, No. 3 (January 1993).

See also Y. Rafferty, *And Miles to Go: Barriers to Academic Achievement and Innovative Strategies for the Delivery of Educational Services to Homeless Children* (New York: Advocates for Children), 1991.

4. Institute for Children and Poverty, "Access to Success."

5. Wood, et al., "Health of Homeless Children and Housed, Poor Children;" Bassuk and Rosenberg, "Psychosocial Characteristics of Homeless Children and Children with Homes;" J. Wagner and E. Menke, "The Mental Health of Homeless Children," paper presented at the annual meeting of the American Public Health Association (New York), September 1990; Bassuk, Rubin and Lauriat, "Characteristics of Sheltered Homeless Families;" Bassuk and Rubin, "Homeless Children;" B. Whitman, *The Crisis in Homelessness: Effect on Children and Families,* testimony presented before the U.S. House of Representatives Select Committee on Children, Youth, and Families (Washington, DC: U.S. Government Printing Office); B. Whitman, P. Accardo, M. Boyert and R. Kendagor, "Homelessness and Cognitive Performance in Children: A Possible Link," unpublished manuscript, Knights of Columbus Developmental Center, Cardinal Glennon Children's Hospital, St. Louis, 1989.

Regarding developmental lags in preschoolers, see Bassuk and Rosenberg, "Why Does Family Homelessness Occur?;" Molnar, *Home is Where the Heart Is;* Bassuk and Rosenberg, "The Psychosocial Characteristics of Homeless and Housed Children."

On the treatment of development problems, see M.E. Walsh, "Developmental and Socio-Emotional Needs of Homeless Infants and Preschoolers," in E.L. Bassuk, R.W. Carman and L.F. Weinreb, eds., *Community Care for Homeless Families: A Program Design Manual* (Newton Centre, MA: The Better Homes Foundation), 1990, pp. 91-100.

6. M.E. Walsh, "Educational and Socio-Emotional Needs of Homeless School-Aged Children," in E.L. Bassuk, R.W. Carman and L.F. Weinreb, eds., *Community Care for Homeless Families: A Program Design Manual* (Newton Centre, MA: The Better Homes Foundation), 1990; D. Wood, J. Ciborowski, B. Ojena and N. Schooler, "Education of Homeless Children and Youth: Problems and Interventions," in E.L. Bassuk, R.W. Carman and L.F. Weinreb, eds., *Community Care for Homeless Families: A Program Design Manual* (Newton Centre, MA: The Better Homes Foundation), 1990.

7. Wood, et al., "Education of Homeless Children and Youth;" Walsh, "Developmental and Socio-Emotional Needs Of Homeless Infants and Preschoolers," pp. 92-95, 104-105.

8. Rafferty, *And Miles to Go*, p. 145.

9. U.S. Department of Education, *1989 Report on Department of Education Activities* (Section 724(b)(2) of P.L. 100-77) and *1989 Status Report on Education of Homeless Children and Youth from State Coordinators* (Section 724(b)(3) of P.L. 100-77) (Washington, DC: U.S. Government Printing Office), March 1990.

On barriers to the education of homeless children, see National Law Center on Homelessness and Poverty, *Shut Out: Denial of Education to Homeless Children* (Washington, DC: National Law Center on Homelessness and Poverty), 1990; Walsh, "Educational and Socio-Emotional Needs of Homeless School-Aged Children," pp. 104-105; Wood, et al., "Education of Homeless Children and Youth," pp. 111-112.

10. On the general state of regulations, see National Law Center for Poverty and Homelessness, *Small Steps: An Update on the Education of Homeless Children and Youth Program* (Washington, DC: National Law Center for Poverty and Homelessness), July 1991, pp. 3-11.

Regarding the McKinney Act, a National Law Center on Homelessness and Poverty study concluded outright that both the Department of Education (DOE) and the states have failed to adequately implement this part of the McKinney Act, that DOE has been lax in distributing funds, providing information, and monitoring state compliance, and that at the local level, state compliance is uneven. It also criticized DOE for interpreting the statute to mean that federal funds could only be used for administrative purposes, and not direct services [this was later clarified in the 1990 amendments]. National Law Center on Homelessness and Poverty, *Shut Out*.

On Texas' state plan, see Wood, et al., "Education of Homeless Children and Youth," p. 113.

11. National Law Center on Homelessness and Poverty, *Small Steps*, p. 4. Regarding the 1990 revision of the McKinney Act, see Center for Law and Education, *Supplement to Materials on the Education of Homeless Children* (Cambridge, MA: Center for Law and Education), May 1991, p. 2; National Law Center on Homelessness and Poverty, *Small Steps*, pp. 6-11.

12. Molnar, *Home is Where the Heart Is*, pp. 1-2; U. Brofenbrenner, *A Report on Longitudinal Evaluations of Early Childhood Programs, Volume 2, Is Early Intervention Effective?*, Department of Health, Education, and Welfare Publication No. OHD 74-24 (Washington, DC: Office of Child Development), 1974; Consortium for Longitudinal Studies, *As the Twig is Bent...Lasting Effects of Preschool Programs* (Hillsdale, NJ: Lawrence Erlbaum Associates), 1983; D.C. Farran, "Effects of Intervention With Disadvantaged and Disabled Children," in S.J. Meisels and J.P. Shonkoff, eds., *Handbook of Early Childhood Intervention* (Oxford: Cambridge University Press), 1990; C. Eliason and L. Jenkins, *A Practical Guide to Early Childhood Curriculum* (St. Louis, MO: The C.V. Mosby Company), 1981, p. 337; A. Henderson, *The Evidence Continues to*

Grow: Parent Involvement Improves Student Achievement (Washington, DC: National Committee for Citizens in Education), 1987.

13. See, for example, Wood, et al., "Education of Homeless Children and Youth," p. 111.

14. Institute for Children and Poverty, "Access to Success," p. 2; U.S. Department of Commerce, Bureau of the Census, *Current Population Reports: School Enrollment: Social and Economic Characteristics of Students: October 1988* (Washington, DC: U.S. Government Printing Office), 1991, p. 19 (Table 4).

15. Ninety-four percent of Head Start programs are part-day, part-year programs. Reich, "What is a Nation?;" National Head Start Association, *Head Start: The Nation's Pride: A Nation's Challenge (1990)*, cited in Child Care Action Campaign, *Where They Stand: A Digest of Organizational Policies on Child Care and Education* (New York: Child Care Action Campaign), March 1993. See also Wood, et al., "Education of Homeless Children and Youth," p. 94.

16. M. Hohmann, B. Banet and D.P. Weikart, *Young Children in Action* (Ypsilanti, MI: High/Scope Press), 1979; D.P. Weikart, L. Rogers, C. Adcock and D. McClelland, *The Cognitively Oriented Curriculum* (Ypsilanti, MI: High/Scope Educational Research Foundation), 1971; W. Fowler, "On the Value of Both Play and Structure in Early Education," *Young Children* 27 (October 1971), pp. 24-36; E.P. Hawkins, *The Logic of Action—Young Children at Work* (New York: Pantheon Books), 1974.

17. For more on the accelerated learning model, see H.M. Levin, "Accelerated Schools for Disadvantaged Students," *Educational Leadership* 44, No. 6 (March 1987), pp. 19-21; H.M. Levin, *Educational Reform for Disadvantaged Students: An Emerging Crisis* (West Haven, CT: NEA Professional Library), 1986; W.S. Hopfenberg, H.M. Levin, G. Meister and J. Rogers, "Towards Accelerated Middle Schools for At-risk Youth," *Report for the Project to Develop Accelerated Middle Schools for Disadvantaged Youth* (Palo Alto, CA: Stanford University), February 1990.

18. Institute for Children and Poverty, "Access to Success," p. 3.

19. Institute for Children and Poverty, "Access to Success," p. 4.

20. Institute for Children and Poverty, "Access to Success," p. 5.

21. Interviews of 68 homeless mothers with school-age children were conducted at HFH RET centers in Summer 1992.

S. Provence and A. Naylor, *Working With Disadvantaged Parents and Their Children* (New Haven, CT: Yale University Press), 1983; J.R. Berrueta-Clement, L.J. Schweinhart, W.S. Barnett, A.S. Epstein and D.P. Weikart, "Changed Lives: The Effects of the Perry Preschool Program on Youths Through Age 19," *Monographs of the High/Scope Educational Research Foundation* (Ypsilanti, MI: High/Scope Press), 1984; E. Galinsky and B. Weissbourd, "Family-Centered Child Care," in B. Spodek and O. Saracho, eds., *Yearbook in Early Childhood, Volume 3: Focusing on Child Care* (New York: Teachers College Press), 1992.

22. Institute for Children and Poverty, "Access to Success," p. 6.

CHAPTER 4

1. Five years ago, over 60 percent of the heads of household held a high school diploma. Today, only 37 percent do. Furthermore, less than half (40 percent) of all family heads have even six months of employment experience, where five years ago some 60 percent could claim at least that amount. Statistics are obtained from intake forms and case notes of families residing in HFH RET Centers. Information was also obtained from structured interviews conducted in 1992 with 596 homeless heads of household at HFH RET Centers. See also Vissing, "Homeless Children Having Children." A 1989 Urban Institute Survey found that 48 percent of homeless adults have not graduated from high school versus 19 percent of all U.S. adults. Burt and Cohen, *America's Homeless.*

2. The National Center for Children in Poverty found in 1992 that children under six whose parents had not completed high school had a poverty rate of 60 percent. By comparison, children under six with high school graduate parents had a poverty rate of 27 percent. Those children whose parents had attended at least some college experienced poverty only 8 percent of the time. For parents who did not receive their high school diploma, the unemployment rate was 39 percent versus only 3 percent for parents with at least some college. National Center for Children in Poverty, *Five Million Children,* p. 6.

Regarding wage levels and education, while the period between 1970 and 1990 brought relative wage decreases for virtually all groups of Americans, the median wage for those with less than a high school education decreased significantly more than the wage for high school graduates (a drop of 27 percent for non-high school graduates versus 18 percent for those who completed high school). Children's Defense Fund, *Leave No Child Behind,* p. 38. Furthermore, employment for the former group is considerably less stable. Both of these problems are even worse for African-Americans than for whites. R. Murnane, "Education and the Well-Being of the Next Generation," paper presented at the national conference of the Institute for Research on Poverty and the Office of the Assistant Secretary for Planning and Evaluation at the U.S. Department of Health and Human Services (University of Wisconsin-Madison), May 28-30, 1992.

It is also worth noting that in 1990, average hourly wages for production or nonsupervisory personnel fell to their lowest point since 1965, and despite the record growth of the 1980's, real hourly wages for production or non-supervisory personnel were lower at the end of the recovery from the 1982 recession than during the recession. This was the first time since record-keeping began in 1947 that wages fell during an economic recovery. Real income fell for the median family with children between 1970 and 1990 (it rose 18 percent for the median childless family). In 1975, the minimum wage provided enough for a family of three to live above the poverty line, but by 1991, a minimum wage job provided only 80 percent of the poverty level. The decline in wages has been worse for young adults as the median hourly wage for 16- to 24-year old men fell 24 percent between 1979 and 1989. Children's Defense Fund, *Leave No Child Behind,* pp. 38-39, 52.

The United States Department of Labor has projected that in the coming years, "many of the jobs in the least skilled job classes will disappear, while positions requiring some technical skills will grow rapidly." The United States Department of Labor also projects that more than half the jobs created by the turn of the century will require education beyond the twelfth grade, and almost one-third of these positions will be filled by people with a college education. Additionally, millions of new workers are lacking even the basic math and communications skills necessary for these kinds of jobs, as shown by a recent National Association of Educational Progress study of 21- to 25-year olds. The Enterprise Foundation (Steven G. Pines), "Employment Strategies for Homeless Families," in E.L. Bassuk, R.W. Carman and L.F. Weinreb, eds., *Community Care for Homeless Families: A Program Design Manual* (Newton Centre, MA: The Better Homes Foundation), 1990, p. 45.

3. The annual median income of working single mothers in the U.S. is $13,092, which is only 33 percent of the $39,895 median income for married-couple families and 37 percent of the $35,353 median income of families generally. U.S. Department of Commerce, U.S. Bureau of the Census, "Money Income of Families, By Type of Family and Income Level: 1990," *Statistical Abstract of the United States: 1992*, 112th Edition (Washington, DC: U.S. Government Printing Office), 1992, p. 452. For more information on the working poor, see S.A. Levitan and I. Shapiro, *Working But Poor* (Baltimore, MD: Johns Hopkins University), 1987.

On the cost of child care, the National Research Council found that parents spend an average of 25 percent of their income on child care. Children's Defense Fund, *Leave No Child Behind*, p. 56. Similarly, the *New York Times* reported that low-income parents spend on average 25 percent of their family income on child care. "For the Children of the Working Poor," *New York Times*, August 23, 1990.

Often, single mothers can only afford child care through child support payments by the father or AFDC. However, only 11 percent of never-married women receive child support payments. Among divorced mothers, only 54 percent actually receive support, even though 82 percent are awarded support by the courts. A 50-state survey of child care for fiscal year 1990 found that child care typically cost $350 per month. Ellwood, *Poor Support*, p. 158; S. Lookner, "FSA and the States," *Child Care Action News* 9, Nos. 5-6 (November-December 1992), p. 4.

A further difficulty in affording quality child care is the "notch" or "cliff" effect. When a family's income rises above the cut-off level for AFDC, the family not only loses its bi-monthly benefits checks, but also the in-kind benefits it received, including child care. Therefore, even a slight rise in income can lead to a huge drop in the standard of living and force a family back on welfare. For more on this issue, see Child Care Action Campaign, *Child Care Action News* 9, Nos. 5-6 (November-December 1992).

On health care costs to low-income families, see Ellwood, *Poor Support*, pp. 105-108; Vissing, "Homeless Children Having Children," p. 395.

A recent study of housing in 44 major cities found that in all but one of these metropolitan areas, at least 50 percent of poor renters spend over half of their income on housing. At least three out of four low-income renters in the nation's largest metropolitan areas spend more on housing than federal standards consider affordable (the federally approved limit is 30 percent of family income). Moreover, for every low-cost rental unit in such cities, there are two households that qualify for it. And only one in three poor urban renters nationwide receives some sort of government housing cost assistance. Center on Budget and Policy Priorities, *The Low Income Housing Crisis in 44 Major Metropolitan Areas* (Washington, DC: Center on Budget and Policy Priorities), 1993.

See also C. Hartman and B. Zigas, "What is Wrong with the Housing Market?," in J.H. Kryder-Coe, L.M. Salamon and J.M. Molnar, eds., *Homeless Children and Youth: A New American Dilemma* (New Brunswick, NJ: Transaction Publishers), 1991; P. Dreier and R. Applebaum, "The Housing Crisis Enters the 1990s," *New England Journal of Public Policy* 8 (Spring-Summer 1992).

4. Students whose parents have less than a high school education consistently scored lower on all levels of math and reading proficiency tests given by the Educational Testing Service and the United States Department of Education than did students whose parents had graduated from high school. Both groups did worse than students with parents having had at least some post-

high school education. Children's Defense Fund, *The Adolescent & Young Adult Fact Book*, p. 107.

For more information on the effects of the primary caregiver's educational attainment on children's educational achievements, see G. Berlin and A. Sum, *Toward a More Perfect Union: Basic Skills, Poor Families and Our Economic Future* (New York: The Ford Foundation), 1988, p. 36; S. Imel, "Adult Literacy Issues: An Update," *ERIC Digest* (89 ED 308 402), p. 4; L.B. Schorr, *Within Our Reach: Breaking the Cycle of Disadvantage* (New York: Doubleday, Anchor Press), 1988, p. 10; D. Harman, *Illiteracy: A National Dilemma* (New York: Cambridge Book Company), 1987, p. 53; T.L. Hibpshman, "An Explanatory Model for Family Literacy Programs," presentation at the Annual Meeting of the Mid-South Educational Research Association, November 1989, p. 1.

On the reluctance of low-income parents to become involved with their child's schooling, see R. Halpern, "Poverty and Early Childhood Parenting: Toward a Framework for Intervention," *American Journal of Orthopsychiatry* 60, No. 1 (January 1990); J. Jones, *Changing Needs for a Changing Future: The Need for Educational Leadership* (New York: National Center for Children in Poverty), 1989.

5. Information was obtained from structured interviews, conducted in the Summer of 1992, with 68 homeless mothers with school-aged children at HFH's RET centers.

See also Jones, *Changing Needs for a Changing Future*, p. 10; J.P. Comer, *School Power* (New York: The Free Press), 1980, p. 127; R. Clark, *Family Life and School Achievement: Why Poor Black Children Succeed or Fail* (Chicago: University of Chicago Press), 1983, p. 206; S. Dauber and J. Epstein, *Parent Attitudes and Practices of Parent Involvement in Inner-City Elementary and Middle Schools* (Baltimore, MD: Center for Research on Elementary and Middle Schools), 1989, p. 21; A. Lareau, "Social Class Differences in Family-School Relationships," p. 79.

6. In FY 1991, 69 percent of congressionally appropriated McKinney funds went toward food and shelter compared to only 3 percent for education and

2 percent for job training. U.S. General Accounting Office, *Homelessness: McKinney Act Programs and Funding Through Fiscal Year 1991* (Washington, DC: U.S. General Accounting Office), December 1992, p. 2.

In 1988, Congress passed the Family Support Act which aimed to start education, job training and employment programs nationwide for welfare recipients. The federal government set certain guidelines, such as exempting women with children under three and providing child and health care and transportation services for up to one year after a family went off AFDC, and provided matching funds to the states. However, many states have not been able or willing to put up the necessary funds. For a description of the Family Support Act see Child Care Action Campaign, "Welfare Reform: Toward Self-sufficiency or Self-destruction?," *Child Care Action News* 9, Nos. 5-6 (November-December 1992). See also S. Blank, R. Collins and S. Smith, *Pathways to Self-Sufficiency for Two Generations* (New York: Foundation for Child Development), 1992, pp. 5-7.

State and local family education programs for low-income people generally are discussed in H. Weiss and R. Halpern, *Community-Based Family Support and Education Programs: Something Old or Something New?* (New York: The National Center for Children in Poverty), 1990, pp. 45-53.

7. See the many studies cited in Weiss and Halpern, *Community-Based Family Support and Education Programs*, pp. 35-36; H. Weiss, "Family Support and Education in Early Childhood Programs," in S. Kagan, D. Powell, B. Weissbourd and E. Zigler, eds., *America's Family Support Programs* (New Haven, CT: Yale University Press), 1987; Molnar, *Home is Where the Heart Is*, pp. 104-105, 86; D. D'Amico Samuels, "Research Review: Adult Learners' Perspectives on Adult Education," *Information Update: New York Literacy Assistance Center* 7, No. 1 (Fall 1990-Winter 1991), pp. 20-23; and G.G. Darkenwald and T. Valentine, "Outcomes of Participation in Adult Basic Skills Education," *Lifelong Learning* 12, No. 1 (September 1988), pp. 17-22; Provence and Naylor, *Working with Disadvantaged Parents and Their Children;* V. Seitz, L. Rosenbaum and N. Apfel, "Effects of Family Support Intervention: A Ten Year Follow-Up," *Child Development* 56 (1985); National Center for Children in Poverty, *Community-Based Family Support and Education Programs;*

Blank, et al., *Pathways to Self-Sufficiency for Two Generations*; Foundation for Child Development and National Center for Children in Poverty, "One Program, Two Generations," *Report on Multidisciplinary Forum on FSA and Effects on At-Risk Children and Their Families* (New York: Foundation for Child Development), 1990.

8. Foundation for Child Development and National Center for Children in Poverty, "One Program, Two Generations." Weiss and Halpern, *Community-Based Family Support and Education Programs*, p. 36.

9. M.L. Gonzalez, "School + Home = A Program for Educating Homeless Students," *Phi Delta Kappan* (June 1990), pp. 785-787; A.T. Henderson, "Good News: An Ecologically Balanced Approach to Academic Improvement," *Educational Horizons* (Winter 1988), p. 62; E. Landerholm and J.A. Karr, "Designing Parent Involvement Program Activities to Deal with Parents' Needs," *Lifelong Learning* 11 (1988), pp. 11-19; N. Radin, "Three Degrees of Maternal Involvement in a Preschool Program: Impact on Mothers and Children," *Child Development* (December 1972), pp. 1355-1364; C. Ascher, "Improving the School-Home Connection for Low-Income Urban Parents," *ERIC Digest Clearinghouse on Urban Education* 41 (March 1988); B.C. Davis, "A Successful Parent Involvement Program," *Educational Leadership* (October 1989), pp. 21-23.

10. J.A. Crandall and S. Imel, "Issues of Adult Literacy Education," *The ERIC Review* 1 (April 1991), pp. 2-7.

11. D.A. Powell, "Parent Education and Support Programs," *ERIC Digest Clearinghouse on Elementary and Early Childhood Education* (1988).

12. B. Goldman, D. Friedlander and D. Long, *Final Report on the San Diego Job Search and Work Experience Demonstration* (New York: Manpower Demonstration Research Corporation), 1986.

   Study by the Urban Institute, cited in National Commission for Employment Policy, *Helping the Homeless Be Choosers: The Role of JTPA in*

Improving Job Prospects, Special Report (Washington, DC: National Commission for Employment Policy), 1990, p. 29.

Fifty-four percent identified educational goals. W. Quinones, "Let Them Have Housing," *New England Journal of Public Policy* 8 (Spring-Summer 1992), p. 575.

13. R.E. Ring, "Massachusetts at a Crossroads," *New England Journal of Public Policy* 8 (Spring-Summer 1992), p. 617.

The National Commission for Employment Policy surveyed Job Training Partnership Act programs in 55 urban locations to determine the accessibility of the programs and their success in meeting the long-term employment needs of the homeless. Over half of the administrators interviewed admitted taking only limited steps to recruit homeless people for their program. Only one-third responded that they provided programs or services targeted for the homeless. National Commission for Employment Policy, *Helping the Homeless Be Choosers*, pp. 37-47. See also S.A. Levitan, "Opportunities for the Working Poor," in S.A. Levitan, ed., *Programs in Aid of the Poor* (Baltimore, MD: Johns Hopkins University Press), 1990.

A 1991 report on the Job Training for the Homeless Demonstration Program, initiated and funded through the McKinney Act of 1987, stated that of the 32 program cites, only 8 specifically targeted their services to a subgroup of the homeless, and then most chose to work with the chronically or severely mentally ill or single adults, not families. U.S. Department of Labor, Employment and Training Administration, *Job Training for the Homeless: Report on the Demonstration's First Year* (Washington, DC: U.S. Government Printing Office), 1991.

14. Many job training courses do not offer work experience as part of the program, often leaving graduates unable to find a job. For more on this and the current disincentives against working in the welfare system, see J. DeParle, "When Giving Up Welfare For a Job Just Doesn't Pay," *New York Times*, July 8, 1992. See also U.S. Department of Labor, *Job Training for the Homeless*.

K. Auletta, *The Underclass* (New York: Vintage Books), 1983; Ellwood, *Poor Support*, pp. 151-155; Kozol, *Rachel and Her Children*, p. 198.

15. A recent study of 255 single-parent families enrolled in California's education and job training program for AFDC recipients (Greater Avenues for Independence, or GAIN) between 1989 and 1991 found that family support issues, particularly lack of child care and personal and family problems, forced many participants to miss portions of the program or drop out altogether. N. Gilbert, J.D. Berrick and M.K. Meyers, *GAIN Family Life and Child Care Study: Final Report* (Berkeley, CA: Family Welfare Research Group), September 1992.

16. Blank, et al., *Pathways to Self-sufficiency for Two Generations*; Child Care Action Campaign, "From Welfare to Work in Denver," *Child Care Action News* 9, Nos. 5-6 (November-December 1992).

CHAPTER 5

1. Wright identifies the following factors that contribute to such poor health: "an uncertain and often inadequate diet and sleeping location, limited or nonexistent facilities for daily hygiene, exposure to elements, direct and constant exposure to the social environment of the streets, communal sleeping and bathing facilities (for those fortunate enough to avail themselves of shelter), unwillingness or inability to follow medical regimens or to seek health care, extended periods on one's feet, an absence of family ties or other social support networks to draw upon in times of illness, extreme poverty (and the consequent absence of health insurance), and a host of related factors." J.D. Wright, "Poverty, Homelessness, Health, Nutrition, and Children," in J.H. Kryder-Coe, L.M. Salamon and J.M. Molnar, eds., *Homeless Children and Youth: A New American Dilemma* (New Brunswick, NJ: Transaction Publishers), 1991, p. 74 (quotation), pp. 71-103 (generally).

See also P.W. Brickner, L.K. Scharer, B. Conanan, A. Elvy and M. Savarese, eds., *Health Care of Homeless People* (New York: Springer), 1985; Institute of Medicine, *Homelessness, Health and Human Needs* (Washington, DC: National Academy Press), 1988; J.D. Wright and P.W. Brickner, "The Health Status of the Homeless: Diverse People, Diverse Problems, Diverse Needs," paper presented at the Annual Meeting of the American Public Health Association

(Washington, DC), November 1985; J.D. Wright and E. Weber, *Homelessness and Health* (New York: McGraw Hill Publishing Company), 1987.

D. Miller and E. Lin, "Children in Sheltered Homeless Families: Reported Health Status and Use of Health Services," *Pediatrics* 81, No. 5 (1988), pp. 668-673.

G. Alperstein, C. Rappaport and J. Flannigan, "Health Problems of Homeless Children in New York City," *American Journal of Public Health* 78, No. 9 (1988), pp. 1232-1233; Bassuk, et al., "Characteristics of Sheltered Homeless Families."

2. Rafferty, "Developmental and Educational Consequences of Homelessness on Children and Youth."

Information was obtained from case records of children in the HFH Child Development Centers and through interviews with HFH daycare teachers and Crisis Nursery staff.

3. L.F. Weinreb and E.L. Bassuk, "Health Programs for Homeless Families," in E.L. Bassuk, R.W. Carman and L.F. Weinreb, eds., *Community Care for Homeless Families: A Program Design Manual* (Newton Centre, MA: The Better Homes Foundation), 1990, pp. 67-82; Burt and Cohen, *America's Homeless*, pp. 48-51; Molnar, *Home is Where the Heart Is*, pp. 70-71; Bassuk, et al., "Characteristics of Sheltered Homeless Families"; R.H. Ropers and R. Boyer, "Homelessness as a Health Risk," *Alcohol World* 11, No. 3 (Spring 1987), p. 41; Burt, *Over the Edge*, pp. 21-24.

4. Burt, *Over the Edge*, p. 109; Burt and Cohen, *America's Homeless*, pp. 48-51; Ropers and Boyer, "Homelessness as a Health Risk," p. 41; Wright and Weber, *Homelessness and Health*, p. 77.

G.R. Garrett, "Homelessness, Alcohol, and Other Drug Abuse: Research Traditions and Policy Responses," *New England Journal of Public Policy* 8 (Spring-Summer 1992), p. 355; P.J. Fischer, "Estimating the Prevalence of Alcohol, Drug and Mental Health Problems in the Contemporary Homeless Population: A Review of the Literature," *Contemporary Drug Problems* 12 (Fall 1989); M.J. Robertson, "Homeless Women with Children: The Role of Alcohol and Other Drug Abuse," *American Psychologist* 46 (1991).

N. Milburn, "Drug Abuse Among the Homeless," in J. Momeni, ed., *Homelessness in the United States: Issues and Data*, Volume 2 (Westport, CT: Greenwood Press), 1990.

B.G. Lubran, "Alcohol Problems Among the Homeless: NIAAA's Response," *Alcohol Health and Research World* 9 (Spring 1987), p. 73.

5. Data was obtained from structured interviews conducted in Summer of 1992 with 596 homeless heads of household at HFH RET centers. The one-third figure may underestimate the percent of homeless parents who are under scrutiny by the CWA, or already have a child in foster care, as the survey did not include women at shelters for singles. Without children, these parents are no longer considered families and are ineligible to live at HFH RET centers, excluding them from the survey.

New York State Coalition for Criminal Justice, *Addicted Mothers, Imprisonment and Alternatives* (Albany, NY: New York State Coalition for Criminal Justice), 1992, p. 11.

Nationally, in 1991, 2.7 million children were reported abused or neglected by their parents, an increase of more than 167 percent since 1979. Of those children, close to half a million were removed from their families and placed in foster care, a 50 percent increase in only five years. Children's Defense Fund, *The State of America's Children*, pp. 62-63.

6. Data is from a study of 246 black children in foster care in New York City and 1003 nationwide. Inadequate housing was a barrier to familial reunification in New York City 45 percent of the time. Black children comprise approximately two-thirds of the foster care population in New York. National Black Child Development Institute, *Who Will Care When Parents Can't?* (Washington, DC: National Black Child Development Institute), 1989, pp. 36, 71, 17, 12; Citizens' Committee for Children, *Keeping Track of New York City's Children* (New York: Citizens' Committee for Children), 1993, p. 128. See also M. Shinn, J.R. Knickman and B.C. Weitzman, "Social Relationships and Vulnerability to Becoming Homeless Among Poor Families," *American Psychologist* 46 (1991), pp. 1180-1187.

D. Knaggs and S. Kelly, *Evaluation of Michigan's Families First Program* (Lansing, MI: University Associates), March 1992. Similarly, a study in Minneapolis found that 38 percent of a sample of homeless people had been in foster care as children. I. Piliavin, M.R. Sosin, and H. Westerfelt, "Tracking the Homeless," *Focus* 10 (1987), pp. 20-25.

Other data was obtained from structured interviews conducted in 1992 with 398 homeless heads of household at HFH RET centers. See also Institute for Children and Poverty, "The New Poverty: A Generation of Homeless Families," *Homes for the Homeless Quarterly Reports* 1, No. 2 (June 1992).

7. Fischer, "Victimization and Homelessness," pp. 232-233.

A study of New York City homeless found that one-fifth of adults had been raped, including two-fifths of the women surveyed. B.E. Jones, B.A. Gray and D.B. Goldstein, "Psychosocial Profiles of the Urban Homeless," in B.E. Jones, ed., *Treating the Homeless: Urban Psychiatry's Challenge* (Washington, DC: American Psychiatric Press), 1986.

Robertson, "Homeless Women with Children."

Additional information was obtained from structured interviews conducted in 1992 with 398 homeless heads of household at HFH RET centers.

8. Children's Defense Fund, *The State of America's Children*, pp. 62-63; Institute for Children and Poverty, "Homelessness: The Foster Care Connection," Homes for the Homeless Quarterly Reports 2, No. 1 (August 1993), p. 1; U.S. Department of Commerce, Bureau of the Census, "Social and Economic Characteristics of the White and Black Populations: 1980-1991," *Statistical Abstract of the United States: 1992*, 112th Edition (Washington, DC: U.S. Government Printing Office), 1992, p. 39.

9. A study of African-American children in New York City's foster care system found that neglect was a primary factor in placement in 65 percent of the cases (abuse constituted 21 percent). National Black Child Development Institute, *Who Will Care When Parents Can't?*, p. 36.

Rossi notes that "the definition of neglect is so unclear that it is doubtful on technical grounds that epidemiological studies of neglect can be undertaken."

P. Rossi, "Evaluating Family Preservation Programs," unpublished report to the Edna McConnell Clark Foundation, Social and Demographic Research Institute. (Amherst, MA), August 1991, p. 9.

C.W. Williams, "Child Welfare Services and Homelessness: Issues in Policy, Philosophy, and Programs," in J.H. Kryder-Coe, L.M. Salamon and J.M. Molnar, eds., *Homeless Children and Youth: A New American Dilemma* (New Brunswick, NJ: Transaction Publishers), 1991, pp. 289-290; Molnar, *Home is Where the Heart Is*, pp. 72-73, 53-55.

Jahiel, "Health and Health Care of Homeless People," pp. 152-159.

10. Williams, "Child Welfare Services and Homelessness, " p. 290. Burt, *Over the Edge*, pp. 21-24, 108-109; Burt and Cohen, *America's Homeless*, pp. 48-51; Ropers and Boyer, "Homelessness as a Health Risk," pp. 41, 89; Molnar, *Home Is Where the Heart Is*, pp. 70-71.

11. C. Zalkind, *Splintered Lives: A Report on Decision Making for Children in Foster Care* (Princeton, NJ: Association for Children), 1988.

Another study of foster care in 5 major cities found that inadequate housing contributed to placement in 30 percent of cases; homelessness, in 8 percent. Inadequate housing was the number one factor that prevented reunification. National Black Child Development Institute, *Who Will Care When Parents Can't?*, pp. 51, 71.

A.L. Dehavenon and M. Boone, *Promises! Promises! Promises! The Failed Hopes of New York City's Homeless Families in 1992* (New York: The Action Research Project on Hunger, Homelessness and Family Health), December 1992, p. 24.

Child Welfare League, *Homelessness: The Impact of Child Welfare in the '90s* (Washington, DC: Child Welfare League of America), December 1990, p. 3.

12. National Black Child Development Institute, *Who Will Care When Parents Can't?*, pp. 30, 40-46.

Child advocates estimate that there are as many as 5,600 homeless former foster care youths in New York City; 1,500 foster care youths "age out" of the system annually. M. Mittelbach, "The Lost Generation," *City Limits* (October 1990).

Institute for Children and Poverty, "Homelessness."

13. For a good discussion of this cycle, see Fischer, "Victimization and Homelessness." See also P.J. Breakey and W.R. Breakey, "Childhood Dysfunction, Homelessness and Mental Health, " paper presented at the World Psychiatric Association Section of Epidemiology and Community Psychiatry Symposium on Psychiatric Epidemiology and Social Science (Oslo, Norway), June 14-16, 1991; E. Susser, E. Struening and S. Conover, "Childhood Experiences of Homeless Men," *American Journal of Psychiatry* 144 (1987), p. 1599-1601; E.L. Struening, D.K. Padgett, S.M. Barrow, P. Cordova, J. Pittman, H. Andrews and M.L. Jones, "Victimization Among Homeless Women and Men," paper presented at the New York State Office of Mental Health Fourth Annual Research Conference (Albany, NY), December 4-6, 1991.

Institute for Children and Poverty, "Homelessness."

14. On the "abundant evidence" that parental visitations "typically rapidly decline in frequency after placement," see D. Fanshel and E.B. Shinn, *Children in Foster Care: A Longitudinal Investigation* (New York: Columbia University Press), 1978.

15. Foster care is not only disruptive, but also considerably more expensive than family preservation. Even the most intensive programs, such as Home Ties in Tennessee where counselors handle only 2 families at a time, only cost $2,255 per child versus the approximately $10,000 it costs the state to maintain a child in foster care for a year. Children's Defense Fund, "Tennessee's Home Ties Keeps Families Together," *CDF Reports* 14, No. 6 (May 1993), p. 3.

In New York City, foster care costs an average of $15,000 per year per child, while family preservation programs only cost an average of $4,500. D. Tobis, "Children on the Brink," *New York Newsday*, July 18, 1991, p. 52. On the argument that foster care is often not in the best interest of a child and should be restricted. See R. Mnookin, "Foster care—In Whose Best Interest?," *Harvard Educational Review* 43 (1973).

CHAPTER 6

1. Dail, "The Psychosocial Context of Homeless Mothers with Young Children," pp. 291-308; New York City Commission on the Homeless, *The Way Home*.

Researchers determined that past shelter use was itself a predictor of future homelessness. Knickman and Weitzman, *A Study of Homeless Families in New York City*, p. 12; Dehavenon and Boone, *Promises! Promises! Promises!* p. 18.

2. In 1989, a full 44 percent of New York City homeless families had never been primary tenants. Only 18 percent of families entering shelters came from their own apartments; 71 percent came from the homes of relatives or friends; and 11 percent had stayed in public places such as hospitals, abandoned buildings, or subways. Knickman and Weitzman, *A Study of Homeless Families in New York City*, pp. 8-9.

3. A. White, "Home Improvement," *City Limits* (April 1993), pp. 14-19.

4. HFH research staff are conducting on-going cohort studies to determine the recidivism rate of formerly homeless families placed in permanent housing and who are no longer on PLUS INC's caseload. Currently, two cohorts totaling 150 families are being traced. Since 1990, several cohorts totaling over 530 families have been tracked.

BIBLIOGRAPHY

PUBLISHED BOOKS AND REPORTS

Auletta, K. *The Underclass.* New York: Vintage Books, 1983.

Bassuk, E.L., Carman, R.W. and Weinreb, L.F., eds. *Community Care for Homeless Families: A Program Design Manual.* Newton Centre, MA: The Better Homes Foundation, 1990.

Berlin, G. and Sum, A. *Toward a More Perfect Union: Basic Skills, Poor Families and Our Economic Future.* New York: The Ford Foundation, 1988.

Berrick, J.D., Gilbert, N. and Meyers, M.K. *GAIN Family Life and Child Care Study: Final Report.* Berkeley, CA: Family Welfare Research Group, September 1992.

The Better Homes Foundation. *Final Report: Evaluation of Programs for Homeless Families.* Newton Centre, MA: The Better Homes Foundation, 1990.

Blank, S., Collins, R. and Smith, S. *Pathways to Self-Sufficiency for Two Generations.* New York: Foundation for Child Development, 1992.

Blau, J. *The Visible Poor: Homelessness in the United States.* New York: Oxford University Press, 1992.

Blumberg, L., Shipley, T., Jr. and Shandler, I.W. *Skid Row and Its Alternatives.* Philadelphia, PA: Temple University Press, 1973.

Bogue, D.B. *Skid Row in American Cities.* Chicago: Community and Family Study Center of the University of Chicago, 1963.

Brickner, P.W., Scharer, L.K., Conanan, B., Elvy, A. and Savarese, M., eds. *Health Care of Homeless People.* New York: Springer Press, 1985.

Burt, M.R. *Over the Edge: The Growth of Homelessness in the 1980s.* New York: Russell Sage Foundation, 1992.

Burt, M.R. and Cohen, B.E. *America's Homeless: Numbers, Characteristics, and the Programs that Serve Them.* Washington, DC: The Urban Institute, 1991.

Burt, M.R. and Cohen, B.E. *State Activities and Programs for the Homeless: A Review of Six States.* Washington, DC: The Urban Institute, 1988.

Center on Budget and Policy Priorities. *End Results: The Impact of Federal Policies Since 1980 on Low-Income Americans.* Washington, DC: Interfaith Action for Economic Justice, September 1984.

Center on Budget and Policy Priorities. *The Low Income Housing Crisis in 44 Major Metropolitan Areas.* Washington, DC: Center on Budget and Policy Priorities, 1993.

Center for Law and Education. *Supplement to Materials on the Education of Homeless Children.* Cambridge, MA: Center for Law and Education, May 1991.

Child Care Action Campaign. *Where They Stand: A Digest of Organizational Policies on Child Care and Education.* New York: Child Care Action Campaign, March 1993.

Child Welfare League of America. *Homelessness: The Impact of Child Welfare in the '90s.* Washington, DC: Child Welfare League of America, December 1990.

Children's Defense Fund. *Leave No Child Behind: An Opinion Maker's Guide to Children in Election Year 1992.* Washington, DC: Children's Defense Fund, 1991.

Children's Defense Fund. *The State of America's Children 1992*. Washington, DC: Children's Defense Fund, 1992.

Citizens' Committee for Children. *Children in Storage: Families in New York City's Barracks-Style Shelters*. New York: Citizens' Committee for Children, 1988.

Citizens' Committee for Children. *Keeping Track of New York City's Children*. New York: Citizens' Committee for Children, 1993.

Citizens' Committee for Children. *On Their Own—At What Cost? A Look at Families Who Leave Shelters*. New York: Citizens' Committee for Children, May 1992.

Clark, R. *Family Life and School Achievement: Why Poor Black Children Succeed or Fail*. Chicago: University of Chicago Press, 1983.

Comer, J.P. *School Power*. New York: The Free Press, 1980.

Consortium for Longitudinal Studies. *As the Twig is Bent...Lasting Effects of Preschool Programs*. Hillsdale, NJ: Lawrence Erlbaum Associates, 1983.

Crouse, J.M. *The Homeless Transient in the Great Depression: New York State, 1929-1941*. Albany, NY: SUNY Press, 1986.

Dauber, S. and Epstein, J. *Parent Attitudes and Practices of Parent Involvement in Inner-City Elementary and Middle Schools*. Baltimore, MD: Center for Research on Elementary and Middle Schools, 1989.

Dehavenon, A.L. and Boone, M. *Promises! Promises! Promises! The Failed Hopes of New York City's Homeless Families in 1992*. New York: The Action Research Project on Hunger, Homelessness and Family Health, December 1992.

Eliason, C. and Jenkins, L. *A Practical Guide to Early Childhood Curriculum*. St. Louis, MO: The C.V. Mosby Company, 1981.

Ellwood, D.T. *Poor Support: Poverty in the American Family*. New York: Basic Books, 1988.

Fanshel, D. and Shinn, E.B. *Children in Foster Care: A Longitudinal Investigation*. New York: Columbia University Press, 1978.

Finlay, B., Simmons, J.M. and Yang, A. *The Adolescent and Young Adult Fact Book*. Washington, DC: Children's Defense Fund, 1991.

Garfinkel, I. and McLanahan, S.S. *Single Mothers And Their Children: A New American Dilemma*. Washington, DC: The Urban Institute Press, 1986.

Garrett, G.R. and Schutt, R.K., eds. *Responding to the Homeless: Policy and Practice*. New York: Plenum Press, 1992.

Gilbert, N., Berrick, J.D. and Meyers, M.K. *GAIN Family Life and Child Care Study: Final Report*. Berkely, CA: Family Welfare Research Group, September 1992.

Goldman, B., Friedlander, D. and Long, D. *Final Report on the San Diego Job Search and Work Experience Demonstration*. New York: Manpower Demonstration Research Corporation, 1986.

Harman, D. *Illiteracy: A National Dilemma*. New York: Cambridge Book Company, 1987.

Hawkins, E.P. *The Logic of Action—Young Children at Work*. New York: Pantheon Books, 1974.

Henderson, A. *The Evidence Continues to Grow: Parent Involvement Improves Student Achievement*. Washington, DC: National Committee for Citizens in Education, 1987.

Hewlett, S.A. *When The Bough Breaks: The Cost Of Neglecting Our Children*. New York: Basic Books, 1991.

Hohmann, M., Banet, B. and Weikart, D.P. *Young Children in Action*. Ypsilanti, MI: High/Scope Press, 1979.

Hopper, K. and Hamberg, J. *The Making of America's Homeless: From Skid Row to New Poor 1945-1984*. New York: Community Service Society, 1984.

Institute of Medicine. *Homelessness, Health and Human Needs*. Washington, DC: National Academy Press, 1988.

Johnson, C.M., Sum, A.M. and Weill, J.D. *Vanishing Dreams: The Growing Economic Plight Of America's Young Families*. Washington, DC: Children's Defense Fund, 1988.

Joint Center for Housing Studies. *The State of the Nation's Housing 1990.* Washington, DC: Joint Center for Housing Studies, 1990.

Jones, J. *Changing Needs for a Changing Future: The Need for Educational Leadership.* New York: National Center for Children in Poverty, 1989.

Klein, T., Bittel, C. and Molnar, J. *No Place to Call Home: Supporting the Needs of Homeless Children in the Early Childhood Classroom.* New York: All Children's House, 1992.

Knaggs, D. and Kelly, S. *Evaluation of Michigan's Families First Program.* Lansing, MI: University Associates Press, March 1992.

Knickman, J.R. and Weitzman, B.C. *A Study of Homeless Families in New York City: Characteristics and Comparisons with Other Public Assistance Families.* New York: Health Research Program of New York University, 1989.

Kozol, J. *Rachel and Her Children.* New York: Crown Publishers, 1988.

Kozol, J. *Savage Inequalities: Children in America's Schools.* New York: Harper Perennial, 1991.

Kryder-Coe, J.H., Salamon, L.M. and Molnar, J.M., eds. *Homeless Children and Youth: A New American Dilemma.* New Brunswick, NJ: Transaction Publishers, 1991.

Levin, H.M. *Educational Reform for Disadvantaged Students: An Emerging Crisis.* West Haven, CT: NEA Professional Library, 1986.

Levitan, S.A. and Shapiro, I. *Working But Poor.* Baltimore, MD: Johns Hopkins University, 1987.

Maza, P.L. and Hall, J.A. *Homeless Children and Their Families: A Preliminary Study.* Washington, DC: Child Welfare League of America, 1988.

Meisels, S.J. and Shonkoff, J.P. *Handbook of Early Childhood Intervention.* Cambridge, MA: Cambridge University Press, 1990.

Mihaly, L.K. *Homeless Families: Failed Policies and Young Victims.* Washington, DC: Children's Defense Fund, January 1991.

Molnar, J.M. *Home is Where the Heart Is: The Crisis of Homeless Children and Families in New York City*. New York: Bank Street College of Education, 1988.

National Alliance to End Homelessness. *Housing and Homelessness*. Washington, DC: National Alliance to End Homelessness, 1988.

National Black Child Development Institute. *Who Will Care When Parents Can't?* Washington, DC: National Black Child Development Institute, 1989.

National Center for Children in Poverty. *Five Million Children: 1992 Update*. New York: Columbia University School of Public Health, 1992.

National Coalition for the Homeless. *Broken Lives: Denial of Education to Homeless Children*. Washington, DC: National Coalition for the Homeless, 1987.

National Coalition for the Homeless. *The Closing Door: Economic Causes of Homelessness*. Washington, DC: National Coalition for the Homeless, 1990.

National Coalition for the Homeless. *Homelessness in the United States: Background and Federal Response. A Briefing Paper for Presidential Candidates*. Washington, DC: National Coalition for the Homeless, 1987.

National Commission for Employment Policy. *Helping the Homeless Be Choosers: The Role of JTPA in Improving Job Prospects*, Special Report. Washington, DC: National Commission for Employment Policy, 1990.

National Head Start Association. *Head Start: The Nation's Pride, A Nation's Challenge*. Alexandria, VA: National Head Start Association, 1990.

National Law Center on Homelessness and Poverty. *Beyond McKinney: Policies to End Homelessness*. Washington, DC: National Law Center on Homelessness and Poverty, November 1992.

National Law Center on Homelessness and Poverty. *Shut Out: Denial of Education to Homeless Children*. Washington, DC: National Law Center on Homelessness and Poverty, 1990.

National Law Center for Poverty and Homelessness. *Small Steps: An Update on the Education of Homeless Children and Youth Program*. Washington, DC: National Law Center on Homelessness and Poverty, July 1991.

Palmer, J.L. and Sawhill, I.F., eds. *The Reagan Record.* Cambridge, MA: Ballinger Publishing Company, 1984.

Parvensky, J. and Krasniewski, D. *In Search of a Place to Call Home: A Profile of Homelessness in Colorado.* Denver, CO: Colorado Coalition for the Homeless, 1988.

Peuquet, S. and Leland, P. *Homelessness in Delware.* Neward, DE: University of Delaware, 1988.

Provence, S. and Naylor, A. *Working With Disadvantaged Parents and Their Children.* New Haven, CT: Yale University Press, 1983.

Rafferty, Y. *And Miles to Go: Barriers to Academic Achievement and Innovative Strategies for the Delivery of Educational Services to Homeless Children.* New York: Advocates for Children, 1991.

Rafferty, Y. and Rollins, N. *Learning in Limbo: The Educational Deprivation of Homeless Children.* New York: Advocates for Children, 1989.

Rossi, P.H. *Down and Out in America: The Origins of Homelessness.* Chicago: University of Chicago Press, 1989.

Rossi, P.H. *The Family, Welfare and Homelessness.* Chicago: University of Chicago Press, 1989.

Rutgers Center for Urban Policy Research. *The Unsheltered Woman: Women and Housing in the '80s.* New Brunswick, NJ: Rutgers Center for Urban Policy Research, 1985.

Schorr, L.B. *Within Our Reach: Breaking the Cycle of Disadvantage.* New York: Doubleday, Anchor Press, 1988.

Schutt, R.K. and Garrett, G.R. *Responsing to the Homeless: Policy and Practice.* New York: Plenum Press, 1992.

Shaw, D., Roberts, C., Nelson, P. and Swaze, B. *Homelessness: A Blight on the American Landscape.* New York: Sage Publishers, 1990.

Simmons, J.M., Finlay, B. and Yang, A. *The Adolescent and Young Adult Fact Book.* Washington, DC: Children's Defense Fund, 1991.

Simpson, J.H., Kilduff, M. and Blewett, C.D. *Struggling to Survive in a Welfare Hotel*. New York: Community Service Society, 1984.

Stanford Center for the Study of Families, Children and Youth. *The Stanford Study of Homeless Families, Children and Youth*. Palo Alto, CA: Stanford Center for the Study of Families, Children and Youth, November 1991.

Torrey, E. F. *Nowhere to Go*. New York: Harper & Row Publishers, 1988.

Walker, L. *Homelessness in the States*. Lexington, KY: Council of State Governments, 1989.

Weikart, D.P., Rogers, L., Adcock, C. and McClelland, D. *The Cognitively Oriented Curriculum*. Ypsilanti, MI: High/Scope Educational Research Foundation, 1971.

Weiss, H. and Halpern, R. *Community-Based Family Support and Education Programs: Something Old or Something New?* New York: The National Center for Children in Poverty, 1990.

Wright, J.D. and Weber, E. *Homelessness and Health*. New York: McGraw-Hill Publishing Company, 1987.

Zalkind, C. *Splintered Lives: A Report on Decision Making for Children in Foster Care*. Princeton, NJ: Association for Children, 1988.

GOVERNMENT DOCUMENTS AND REPORTS

Brofenbrenner, U. *A Report on Longitudinal Evaluations of Early Childhood Programs, Volume 2, Is Early Intervention Effective?* Department of Health, Education, and Welfare Publication No. OHD 74-24. Washington, DC: Office of Child Development, 1974.

Interagency Council on the Homeless. *Federal Progress Toward Ending Homelessness*. Washington, DC: Interagency Council on the Homeless, September 1992.

Interagency Council on the Homeless. "How Many Homeless People Are There?" *Fact Sheet*, April 1991.

Interagency Council on the Homeless. "How Much is the Federal Government Spending on Programs to Help the Homeless?" *Fact Sheet*, April 1992.

Interagency Council on the Homeless. *The McKinney Act: A Program Guide.* Washington, DC: Interagency Council on the Homeless, January 1992.

National Commission on Children. *Beyond Rhetoric: A New American Agenda for Children and Families.* Washington, DC: U.S. Government Printing Office, 1991.

New York City Commission on the Homeless. *The Way Home: A New Direction in Social Policy.* New York: New York City Commission on the Homeless, 1992.

New York City Human Resources Administration, Adult Services Administration, Bureau of Management Information Systems. *Emergency Housing Services for Homeless Families: Monthly Report.* New York: New York City Human Resources Administration, May 1993.

New York City Human Resources Administration, Adult Services Administration, Bureau of Management Information Systems. *Update to the Single and Family Shelter Statistics.* New York: New York City Human Resources Administration, March 1991.

New York City Office of the Mayor, David N. Dinkins. *Revised and Updated Plan for Housing and Assisting Homeless Single Adults and Families.* New York: New York City Mayor's Office on Homelessness and SRO Housing, March 1993.

Reyes, L.M. and Waxman, L.D. *Status Report on Hunger and Homelessness in America's Cities, 1989: A 27-City Survey.* Washington, DC: U.S. Conference of Mayors, 1989.

U.S. Advisory Board on Child Abuse and Neglect. *Child Abuse and Neglect: Critical First Steps in Response to a National Emergency.* Washington, DC: U.S. Department of Health and Human Services, August 1990.

U.S. Conference of Mayors. *Status Report on Homeless Families in America's Cities: A 29-City Survey.* Washington, DC: U.S. Conference of Mayors, May 1987.

U.S. Conference of Mayors. *Status Report On Hunger and Homelessness in America's Cities: A 29-City Survey.* Washington, DC: U.S. Conference of Mayors, December 1990.

U.S. Conference of Mayors. *Status Report on the Stewart B. McKinney Homeless Assistance Act of 1987.* Washington, DC: U.S. Conference of Mayors, June 1988.

U.S. Congress. *Stewart B. McKinney Homelessness Assistance Act*. Public Law 100-77 July 2, 1987, codified as 42 U.S.C. SS11301-11472.

U. S. Department of Commerce, Bureau of the Census. *Current Population Reports: School Enrollment: Social and Economic Characteristics of Students: October 1988*. Washington, DC: U.S. Government Printing Office, 1991.

U.S. Department of Commerce, Bureau of the Census. "Money Income of Families, By Type of Family and Income Level: 1990." In *Statistical Abstract of the United States: 1992*, 112th Edition. Washington, DC: U.S. Government Printing Office, 1992.

U.S. Department of Commerce, Bureau of the Census. "Social and Economic Characteristics of the White and Black Populations: 1980-1991." In *Statistical Abstract of the United States: 1992*, 112th Edition. Washington, DC: U.S. Government Printing Office, 1992.

U.S. Department of Education. *1989 Report on Department of Education Activities*. Section 724b2 of P.L. 100-77. Washington, DC: U.S. Government Printing Office, 1990.

U.S. Department of Education. *1989 Status Report on Education of Homeless Children and Youth from State Coordinators*. Section 724b3 of P.L. 100-77. Washington, DC: Government Printing Office, March 1990.

U.S. Department of Education. *Report to Congress: State Interim Report on the Education of Homeless Children*. Washington, DC: U.S. Government Printing Office, 1985.

U.S. Department of Education. *Report to Congress: State Interim Report on the Education of Homeless Children*. Washington, DC: U.S. Government Printing Office, 1989.

U.S. Department of Health and Human Services, National Center for Health Statistics. *Vital Statistics of the United States*. Washington, DC: U.S. Government Printing Office, 1990.

U.S. Department of Housing and Urban Development. *Homeless Assistance Policy and Practice in the Nation's Five Largest Cities*. Washington, DC: U.S. Department of Housing and Urban Development, 1989.

U.S. Department of Housing and Urban Development, Office of Policy Development and Research. *A Report to the Secretary on the Homeless and Emergency Shelters.* Washington, DC: Department of Housing and Urban Development, 1984.

U.S. Department of Labor, Employment and Training Administration. *Job Training for the Homeless: Report on the Demonstration's First Year.* Washington, DC: U.S. Government Printing Office, 1991.

U.S. General Accounting Office. *Homelessness: Access to McKinney Act Programs Improved But Better Oversight Needed.* GAO/RCED-91-29. Washington, DC: U.S. General Accounting Office, December 1990.

U.S. General Accounting Office. *Homelessness: McKinney Act Programs and Funding Through Fiscal Year 1991.* GAO/RCED-93-39. Washington, DC: U.S. General Accounting Office, December 1992.

U.S. General Accounting Office. *Homelessness: Transitional Housing Shows Initial Success But Long-Term Effects Unknown.* GAO/RCED-91-200. Washington, DC: U.S. General Accounting Office, September 1991.

U.S. House of Representatives, Committee on Ways and Means. *Background Material And Data On Programs Within The Jurisdiction Of The Committee On Ways And Means.* Washington, DC: U.S. Government Printing Office, 1989.

U.S. House of Representatives, Committee on Ways and Means. *Overview of Entitlement Programs: The 1990 Green Book.* Washington, DC: U.S. Government Printing Office, 1990.

Wasem, R. *Homelessness: Issues and Legislation in 1988.* Washington, DC: Congressional Research Service, 1988.

Whitman, B. "The Crisis in Homelessness: Effect on Children and Families." Testimony presented before the U.S. House of Representatives Select Committee on Children, Youth, and Families. Washington, DC: U.S. Government Printing Office, 1987.

Wood, D., Hayashi, T., Schlossman, K. and Valdez, R.B. *Over the Brink: Homeless Families in Los Angeles.* Sacramento, CA: California Assembly Office of Research, 1989.

ARTICLES IN JOURNALS AND ANTHOLOGIES

Alperstein, G., Rappaport, C. and Flannigan, J. "Health Problems of Homeless Children in New York City." *American Journal of Public Health* 78, No. 9, 1988.

Argeriou, M. "Homelessness in Massachusetts: Perception, Policy, and Progress." *New England Journal of Public Policy* 8, Spring-Summer 1992.

Ascher, C. "Improving the School-Home Connection for Low-Income Urban Parents." *ERIC Digest Clearinghouse on Urban Education* 41, March 1988.

Bassuk, E.L. "The Problem of Family Homelessness." In *Community Care for Homeless Families: A Program Design Manual.* Bassuk, E.L., Carman, R.W. and Weinreb, L.F., eds. Newton Centre, MA: The Better Homes Foundation, 1990.

Bassuk, E.L. and Rosenberg, L. "Psychosocial Characteristics of Homeless Children and Children With Homes." *Pediatrics* 85, 1990.

Bassuk, E.L. and Rosenberg, L. "Why Does Family Homelessness Occur? A Case-Control Study." *American Journal of Public Health* 78, July 1988.

Bassuk, E.L. and Rubin, L. "Homeless Children: A Neglected Population." *American Journal of Orthopsychiatry* 57, 1987.

Bassuk, E.L., Rubin, L. and Lauriat, A.S. "Characteristics of Sheltered Homeless Families." *American Journal of Public Health* 76, September 1986.

Bassuk, E.L. and Wallace, R. "Housing Famine and Homelessness: How the Low-Income Housing Crisis Affects Families with Inadequate Supports." *Environment and Planning* 23, 1991.

Berrueta-Clement, J.R., Schweinhart, L.J., Barnett, W.S., Epstein, A.S. and Weikart, D.P. "Changed Lives: The Effects of the Perry Preschool Program on Youths Through Age 19." In *Monographs of the High/Scope Educational Research Foundation.* Schweinhart, L.J., Barnes, H.V. and Weikart, D.P., eds. Ypsilanti, MI: High/Scope Press, 1984.

Birch, E.L. "The Unsheltered Woman: Definition and Needs." In *The Unsheltered Woman: Women and Housing in the '80s.* New Brunswick, NJ: Rutgers Center for Urban Policy Research, 1985.

Chavkin, W., Kristal, A., Seabron, C. and Guigli, P.E. "Reproductive Experience of Women Living in Hotels for the Homeless in New York City." *New York State Journal of Medicine* 87, 1987.

Child Care Action Campaign. "From Welfare to Work in Denver." *Child Care Action News* 9, Nos. 5-6, November-December 1992.

Child Care Action Campaign. "Welfare Reform: Toward Self-Sufficiency or Self-Destruction?" *Child Care Action News* 9, Nos. 5-6, November-December 1992.

Children's Defense Fund. "Births to Teens." *CDF Reports* 14, No. 7, June 1993.

Children's Defense Fund. "Tennessee's Home Ties Keeps Families Together." *CDF Reports* 14, No. 6, May 1993.

Crandall, J. and Imel, S. "Issues of Adult Literacy Education." *The ERIC Review* 1, April 1991.

Dail, P.W. "The Psychosocial Context of Homeless Mothers with Young Children: Program and Policy Implications." *Child Welfare* 69, July-August 1990.

D'Amico Samuels, D. "Research Review: Adult Learners' Perspectives on Adult Education." *Information Update: New York Literacy Assistance Center* 7, No. 1, Fall 1990-Winter 1991.

Darkenwald, G.G. and Valentine, T. "Outcomes of Participation in Adult Basic Skills Education." *Lifelong Learning* 12, No. 1, September 1988.

Davis, B.C. "A Successful Parent Involvement Program." *Educational Leadership*, October 1989.

DeParle, J. "When Giving Up Welfare For a Job Just Doesn't Pay." *New York Times*, July 8, 1992.

Dreier, P. and Applebaum, R. "The Housing Crisis Enters the 1990s." *New England Journal of Public Policy* 8, Spring-Summer 1992.

Enterprise Foundation (Steven G. Pines). "Employment Strategies for Homeless Families." In *Community Care for Homeless Families: A Program Design Manual*, Bassuk, E.L., Carman, R.W. and Weinreb, L.F. Newton Centre, MA: The Better Homes Foundation, 1990.

Farran, D.C. "Effects of Intervention With Disadvantaged and Disabled Children." In *Handbook of Early Childhood Intervention*. Meisels, S.J. and Shonkoff, J.P., eds. Oxford: Cambridge University Press, 1990.

Fischer, P.J. "Estimating the Prevalence of Alcohol, Drug and Mental Health Problems in the Contemporary Homeless Population: A Review of the Literature." *Contemporary Drug Problems* 12, Fall 1989.

Fischer, P.J. "Victimization and Homelessness." *New England Journal of Public Policy* 8, Spring-Summer 1992.

"For the Children of the Working Poor." *New York Times*, August 23, 1990.

Foundation for Child Development and National Center for Children in Poverty. "One Program, Two Generations." In *Report on Multidisciplinary Forum on FSA and Effects on At-Risk Children and Their Families*. New York: Foundation for Child Development, 1990.

Fowler, W. "On the Value of Both Play and Structure in Early Education." *Young Children* 27, October 1971.

Galinsky, E. and Weissbourd, B. "Family-Centered Child Care." In *Yearbook in Early Childhood, Volume 3: Focusing on Child Care*. Spodek, B. and Saracho, O., eds. New York: Teachers College Press, 1992.

Garrett, G.R. "Homelessness, Alcohol, and Other Drug Abuse: Research Traditions and Policy Responses." *New England Journal of Public Policy* 8, Spring-Summer, 1992.

Gonzalez, M. "School + Home = A Program for Educating Homeless Students." *Phi Delta Kappa*, June 1990.

Greenblatt, M. "Deinstitutionalization and Reinstitutionalization of the Mentally Ill." In *Homelessness: A National Perspective*. Robertson, M.J. and Greenblatt, M., eds. New York: Plenum Press, 1992.

Halpern, R. "Poverty and Early Childhood Parenting: Toward a Framework for Intervention." *American Journal of Orthopsychiatry* 60, No. 1, January 1990.

Hartman, C. and Zigas, B. "What is Wrong with the Housing Market?" In *Homeless Children and Youth: A New American Dilemma*. Kryder-Coe, J.H., Salamon, L.M. and Molnar, J.M., eds. New Brunswick, NJ: Transaction Publishers, 1991.

Henderson, A.T. "Good News: An Ecologically Balanced Approach to Academic Improvement." *Educational Horizons*, Winter 1988.

Hope, M. and Young, J. "From Back Wards to Back Alleys: Deinstitutionalization and the Homeless." *Urban and Social Change Review* 17, 1984.

Hopfenberg, W.S., Levin, H.M., Meister, G. and Rogers, J. "Towards Accelerated Middle Schools for At-risk Youth." In *Report for the Project to Develop Accelerated Middle Schools for Disadvantaged Youth.* Palo Alto, CA: Stanford University Press, February 1990.

Imel, S. "Adult Literacy Issues: An Update." *ERIC Digest*, 89 ED 308 402, 1989.

Institute for Children and Poverty. "Access to Success: Meeting the Educational Needs of Homeless Children and Their Families." *Homes for the Homeless Quarterly Reports* 1, No. 3, January 1993.

Institute for Children and Poverty. "Homelessness: The Foster Care Connection." *Homes for the Homeless Quarterly Reports* 2, No. 1, August 1993.

Institute for Children and Poverty. "The New Poverty: A Generation of Homeless Families." *Homes for the Homeless Quarterly Reports* 1, No. 2, June 1992.

Jahiel, R.I. "Health and Health Care of Homeless People." In *Homelessness: A National Perspective*. Robertson, M.J. and Greenblatt, M., eds. New York: Plenum Press, 1992.

Jones, B.E., Gray, B.A. and Goldstein, D.B. "Psychosocial Profiles of the Urban Homeless." In *Treating the Homeless: Urban Psychiatry's Challenge*. Jones, B.E., ed. Washington, DC: American Psychiatric Press, 1986.

Jordan, M. "Issues That Won't Go Away." *America's Agenda*, Spring 1993.

Kasarda, J.D. "Jobs, Migration, And Emerging Urban Mismatches." In *Urban Change and Poverty*. McGeary, M.G.H. and Lynn, L.E., Jr., eds. Washington, DC: National Academy Press, 1988.

Kaufman, N.K. "State Government's Response to Homelessness: The Massachusetts Experience, 1983-1990." *New England Journal of Public Policy* 8, Spring-Summer 1992.

Kerr, R.D. "Shelter the American Way: Federal Urban Housing Policy, 1900-1980." *New England Journal of Public Policy* 8, Spring-Summer 1992.

Kirchheimer, D.W. "Sheltering the Homeless in New York City: Expansion in an Era of Government Expansion." *Political Science Quarterly* 104, 1989-1990.

Klein, T.P., Molnar, J.M. and Rath, W.R. "Constantly Compromised: The Impact of Homelessness on Children." *Journal of Social Issues* 46, 1990.

Landerholm, E. and Karr, J.A. "Designing Parent Involvement Program Activities to Deal with Parents' Needs." *Lifelong Learning* 11, 1988.

Lareau, A. "Social Class Differences in Family-School Relationships: The Importance of Cultural Capital." *Sociology of Education* 60, April 1987.

Lauriat, A.S. "Sheltering Homeless Families: Beyond An Emergency Response." In *The Mental Health Needs of Homeless Persons*. Bassuk, E.L., ed. San Francisco, CA: Jossey-Bass, 1986.

Leavitt, J. "Homelessness and the Housing Crisis." In *Homelessness: A National Perspective*. Robertson, M.J. and Greenblatt, M., eds. New York: Plenum Press, 1992.

Levin, H.M. "Accelerated Schools for Disadvantaged Students." *Educational Leadership* 44, No. 6, March 1987.

Levitan, S.A. "Opportunities for the Working Poor." In *Programs in Aid of the Poor*. Levitan, S.A., ed. Baltimore, MD: Johns Hopkins University Press, 1990.

Lookner, S. "FSA and the States." *Child Care Action News* 9, Nos. 5-6, November-December 1992.

Lubran, B.G. "Alcohol Problems Among the Homeless: NIAAA's Response." *Alcohol Health and Research World* 9, Spring 1987.

Martin, J. "The Trauma of Homelessness." *International Journal of Mental Health* 20, 1991.

McCambridge, R. and Robb, N. "Private Funders: Their Role in Homelessness Projects." *New England Journal of Public Policy* 8, Spring-Summer 1992.

McChesney, K.Y. "Macroeconomic Issues in Poverty: Implications for Child and Youth Homelessness." In *Homeless Children and Youth: A New American Dilemma*. Kryder-Coe, J.H., Salamon, L.M. and Molnar, J.M., eds. New Brunswick, NJ: Transaction Publishers, 1991.

McChesney, K.Y. "New Findings on Homeless Families." *Family Professional* 1, 1986.

Merves, E.S. "Homeless Women: Beyond the Bag Lady Myth." In *Homelessness: A National Perspective*. Robertson, M.J. and Greenblatt, M., eds. New York: Plenum Press, 1992.

Milburn, N. "Drug Abuse Among the Homeless." In *Homelessness in the United States: Issues and Data*, Volume 2. Momeni, J., ed. Westport, CT: Greenwood Press, 1990.

Miller, D. and Lin, E. "Children in Sheltered Homeless Families: Reported Health Status and Use of Health Services." *Pediatrics* 81, No. 5, 1988.

Mills, C. and Ota, H. "Homeless Women with Minor Children in the Detroit Metropolitan Area." *Social Work* 34, 1989.

Mittelbach, M. "The Lost Generation." *City Limits*, October 1990.

Mnookin, R. "Foster Care—In Whose Best Interest?" *Harvard Educational Review* 43, 1973.

Molnar, J.M., Rath, W.R. and Klein, T.P. "Constantly Compromised: The Impact of Homelessness on Children." *Journal of Social Issues* 46, 1990.

National Alliance to End Homelessness. "Budget Figures for Fiscal Year 1994." *Alliance* 9, May 1993.

National Alliance to End Homelessness. "National Groups Brief Congressional Staff on Solutions to Homelessness." *Alliance* 9, May 1993.

New York State Coalition for Criminal Justice. *Addicted Mothers, Imprisonment and Alternatives*. Albany, NY: New York State Coalition for Criminal Justice, 1992.

Piliavin, I., Sosin, M.R. and Westerfelt, H. "Tracking the Homeless." *Focus* 10, 1987.

Powell, D.A. "Parent Education and Support Programs." *ERIC Digest Clearinghouse on Elementary and Early Childhood Education,* 1988.

Quinones, W. "Let Them Have Housing." *New England Journal of Public Policy* 8, Spring-Summer 1992.

Radin, N. "Three Degrees of Maternal Involvement in a Preschool Program: Impact on Mothers and Children." *Child Development,* December 1972.

Rafferty, Y. "Developmental and Educational Consequences of Homelessness on Children and Youth." In *Homeless Children and Youth: A New American Dilemma.* Kryder-Coe, J.H., Salamon, L.M. and Molnar, J.M., eds. New Brunswick, NJ: Transaction Publishers, 1991.

Rafferty, Y. and Shinn, M. "The Impact of Homelessness on Children." *American Psychologist* 46, 1991.

Reich, R.B. "As the World Turns." *New Republic* 3876, 1989.

Reich, R.B. "What is a Nation?" *Political Science Quarterly* 106, 1991.

Ring, R. E. "Massachusetts at a Crossroads." *New England Journal of Public Policy* 8, Spring-Summer 1992.

Robb, N. and McCambridge, R. "Private Funders: Their Role in Homelessness Projects." *New England Journal of Public Policy* 8, Spring-Summer 1992.

Robertson, M.J. "Homeless Women with Children: The Role of Alcohol and Other Drug Abuse." *American Psychologist* 46, 1991.

Ropers, R.H. and Boyer, R. "Homelessness as a Health Risk." *Alcohol World* 11, No. 3, Spring 1987.

Rossi, P.H. "The Old Homeless And New Homeless In Historical Perspective." *American Psychologist* 45, August 1990.

Seitz, V., Rosenbaum, L. and Apfel, N. "Effects of Family Support Intervention: A Ten Year Follow-up." *Child Development* 56, 1985.

Shinn, M., Knickman, J.R. and Weitzman, B.C. "Social Relationships and Vulnerability to Becoming Homeless Among Poor Families." *American Psychologist* 46, 1991.

Solarz, A. L. "To Be Young and Homeless: The Implications of Homelessness for Children." In *Homelessness: A National Perspective*. Robertson, M.J. and Greenblatt, M., eds. New York: Plenum Press, 1992.

Stegman, M.A. "Remedies for Homelessness: An Analysis of Potential Housing Policy and Program Responses." In *Homeless Children and Youth: A New American Dilemma*. Kryder-Coe, J.H., Salamon, L.M. and Molnar, J.M., eds. New Brunswick, NJ: Transaction Publishers, 1991.

Stoner, M.R. "The Plight of the Homeless Woman." In *Housing the Homeless*. Erickson, J. and Wilhelm, C., eds. New York: Center for Urban Policy Research, 1984.

Susser, E., Struening, E. and Conover, S. "Childhood Experiences of Homeless Men." *American Journal of Psychiatry* 144, 1987.

Tobis, D. "Children on the Brink." *New York Newsday*, July 18, 1991.

Tull, J. "Homelessness: An Overview." *New England Journal of Public Policy* 8, Spring-Summer 1992.

Vissing, Y.M. "Homeless Children Having Children." *New England Journal of Public Policy* 8, Spring-Summer 1992.

Walker, L. "HUD's Administration of the McKinney Act: A Problem of State-Federal Relations." *The Journal of State Government* 63, January-March 1990.

Wallace, R. and Bassuk, E. "Housing Famine and Homelessness: How the Low-Income Housing Crisis Affect Families with Inadequate Supports." *Environment and Planning* 23, 1991.

Walsh, M.E. "Developmental and Socio-Emotional Needs of Homeless Infants and Preschoolers." In *Community Care for Homeless Families: A Program Design Manual*. Bassuk, E.L., Carman, R.W. and Weinreb, L.F., eds. Newton Centre, MA: The Better Homes Foundation, 1990.

Walsh, M.E. "Educational and Socio-Emotional Needs of Homeless School-Aged Children." In *Community Care for Homeless Families: A Program Design*

Manual. Bassuk, E.L., Carman, R.W. and Weinreb, L.F., eds. Newton Centre, MA: The Better Homes Foundation, 1990.

Weinreb, L.F. and Bassuk, E.L. "Health Programs for Homeless Families." In *Community Care for Homeless Families: A Program Design Manual*. Bassuk, E.L., Carman, R.W. and Weinreb, L.F., eds. Newton Centre, MA: The Better Homes Foundation, 1990.

Weiss, H. "Family Support and Education in Early Childhood Programs." In *America's Family Support Programs*. Kagan, S., Powell, D., Weissbourd, B. and Zigler, E., eds. New Haven, CT: Yale University Press, 1987.

White, A. "Home Improvement." *City Limits*, April 1993.

Williams, C.W. "Child Welfare Services and Homelessness: Issues in Policy, Philosophy, and Programs." In *Homeless Children and Youth: A New American Dilemma*. Kryder-Coe, J.H., Salamon, L.M. and Molnar, J.M., eds. New Brunswick, NJ: Transaction Publishers, 1991.

Wood, D., Ciborowski, J., Ojena, B. and Schooler, N. "Education of Homeless Children and Youth." In *Community Care for Homeless Families: A Program Design Manual*. Bassuk, E.L., Carman, R.W. and Weinreb, L.F., eds. Newton Centre, MA: The Better Homes Foundation, 1990.

Wood, D.L., Valdez, R.B. and Shen, A. "Health of Homeless Children and Housed, Poor Children." *Pediatrics* 86, 1990.

Wright, J.D. "Poverty, Homelessness, Health, Nutrition, and Children." In *Homeless Children and Youth: A New American Dilemma*. Kryder-Coe, J.H., Salamon, L.M. and Molnar, J.M., eds. New Brunswick, NJ: Transaction Publishers, 1991.

Zuckman, J. "The Next Education Crisis: Equalizing School Funds." *Congressional Quarterly Weekly Report* 51, March 27, 1993.

UNPUBLISHED MATERIALS

Accardo, P., Boyert, M., Kendagor, R. and Whitman, B. "Homelessness and Cognitive Performance in Children: A Possible Link." Unpublished manuscript, Knights of Columbus Developmental Center, Cardinal Glennon Children's Hospital, St. Louis, MO, 1989.

Breakey, P.J. and Breakey, W.R. "Childhood Dysfunction, Homelessness and Mental Health." Paper presented at the World Psychiatric Association Section of Epidemiology and Community Psychiatry Symposium on Psychiatric Epidemiology and Social Science, Oslo, Norway, June 14-16, 1991.

Friedmutter, C. "Service-Enriched Housing for Homeless Families." Unpublished report prepared for the Robert Wood Johnson Foundation, Princeton, NJ, February 1989.

Hibpshman, T.L. "An Explanatory Model for Family Literacy Programs." Presentation at the Annual Meeting of the Mid-South Educational Research Association, November 1989.

Horsey, C. "Is the Family Ready for School? Is the School Ready for the Family?" Unpublished report, Homes for the Homeless, New York, August 1991.

Interviews, 596 homeless heads-of-household at Homes for the Homeless RET centers, Homes for the Homeless, New York, 1992.

Menke, E. and Wagner, J. "The Mental Health of Homeless Children." Paper presented at the annual meeting of the American Public Health Association, New York, September 1990.

Murnane, R. "Education and the Well-Being of the Next Generation." Paper presented at the national conference of the Institute for Research on Poverty and the Office of the Assistant Secretary for Planning and Evaluation at the U.S. Department of Health and Social Services, University of Wisconsin-Madison, May 28-30, 1992.

Rossi, P. "Evaluating Family Preservation Programs." Unpublished report, Social and Demographic Research Institute, Amherst, MA, for the Edna McConnell Clark Foundation, August 1991.

Struening, E.L., Padgett, D.K., Barrow, S.M., Cordova, P., Pittman, J., Andrews, H. and Jones, M.L. "Victimization Among Homeless Women and Men." Paper presented at the New York State Office of Mental Health Fourth Annual Research Conference, Albany, NY, December 4-6, 1991.

Wagner, J. and Menke, E. "The Mental Health of Homeless Children." Paper presented at the annual meeting of the American Public Health Association, New York, September 1990.

Whitman, B., Accardo, P., Boyert, M. and Kendagor, R. "Homelessness and Cognitive Performance in Children: A Possible Link." Unpublished manuscript, Knights of Columbus Departmental Center, Cardinal Glennon Children's Hospital, St. Louis, 1989.

Wright, J.D. and Brickner, P.W. "The Health Status of the Homeless: Diverse People, Diverse Problems, Diverse Needs." Paper presented at the Annual Meeting of the American Public Health Association, Washington, DC, November 1985.

INDEX

Adult education,
  of the homeless, 51, 95-122
Adult Education Centers,
  at RET centers, 102-106
Aftercare programs, 155-157
Afterschool programs,
  at RET centers, 51
Aid to Families with Dependent
  Children (AFDC)
  Emergency Assistance funding
  stream, 185-186
  federal cuts in, 20, 21 (fig.)
Alternative High Schools, 52, 102, 115
  results of, 121

Barnes v. Koch, 181
Barnett, Helaine, 5, 186
Brezenoff, Stanley, 7
Brownstone School, 51, 75-78
  results of, 87-92, 90 (fig.), 91 (fig.)
Bush, George, 15

Camp Kiwago, 82-83
Camp Lanowa, 82-83
Caseworkers, at RET centers,
  51, 106, 163
Cathedral of St. John the Divine, 6-7
Child abuse, 129-132
Child care, 117
Child Development Centers (CDCs),
  74-75, 103
  results of, 83
Child neglect, 132
Child Welfare Agency, New York City,
  cases involving the homeless, 127,
  133 (fig.)
Children
  educational status of homeless vs.
  non-homeless, 63 (fig.)
  poverty rates for, 11-13, 12 (fig.)
  See also Children, homeless
Children, homeless
  academic gains, 90 (fig.)

Children, homeless-continued
  demographic profile of, 59 (table)
  developmental gains, 86 (fig.)
  educational and recreational
    programs for, at RET centers, 51,
    70-83, 87-93
  educational deprivation of, 62-68
  effects of homelessness on, 8,
    33-34, 41
  foster care prevention programs,
    126, 146
  health problems of, 126
  mental health problems of,
    126-127
  school attendance rates, 58-62,
    91 (fig.)
Clinton RET center, 50, 149
Cosentino v. Perales, 182
Counseling, at RET centers, 52
Crisis nurseries, 139-143
  events triggering use of, 142 (fig.)
  See also Family Crisis Nursery
Cuomo, Governor Mario, 5

D & Z Holding Corp. v. The City of
  New York, 183-184
Dinkins, Mayor David, 34
Domestic violence, among homeless
  parents, 33, 129

East Harlem School of Music, 82
Education
  effect of homelessness on, 62-68
  federal spending cuts in, 20
  of homeless parents, 95-122
  as key to overcoming poverty and
    homelessness, 57-93
  programs at RET centers, 51-52,
    68-70, 74-78, 87-92
  remedial vs. accelerated, 69, 75
El Grupo Morivivi, 82
Emergency Assistance (AFDC),
  185-186
Emergency Assistance Units
  (NewYork City), 5-6
Emmett, William, 5

Employment trends, 96-97
English as a Second Language (ESL)
  at RET centers, 103

Families, single-female-headed,
  18 (fig.)
Family-based support, 117-120
Family Crisis Nursery (HFH),
  53, 137, 139-143
  costs of, vs. foster care, 149-150
  results of, 149
Family education
  of the homeless, 52, 95-122
Family health programs, 52-53
Family Preservation and Reunification
  Program (HFH), 53, 137, 146
  results of, 149
Family preservation programs,
  52-53, 125-151
Family rights litigation in New York
  City, history of, 177-184
Federal spending
  for adult education and job training
    of homeless, 100
  for AFDC, 20, 21 (fig.)
  for education, 20
  for housing assistance, 16 (fig.), 17
  for social programs, 17-20, 19 (fig.)
Fieldworkers, RET center, 167
Food Stamp Program, 20
Foster care
  costs of, vs. proactive family
    programs, 149-150, 151 (table)
  homeless parents with history of,
    profile, 136 (fig.)
  increase in, in New York, 126-134,
    130 (fig.)
  link with poverty, 134-135
  prevention programs, 126, 146
  problems of, 134-137, 149-150
Fulton v. Krauskopf, 182

General Equivalency Diploma (GED),
  52, 92, 102, 115
Gonzalez v. Martinique Hotel
  Affiliates, 181

Hamilton Place Associates v.
  City of New York, 184
Hartz Mountain Corporation, 7
Head Start, 70
Health care, for the homeless, 52,
  33, 125-127, 138-139
Health problems, of homeless
  children, 126
Healthy Living Centers (HFH), 51,
  78-83, 92, 139
High/Scope curriculum, 74
Holloway, Ben, 6
Home-based services, 53
Homeless, the
  adult education for, 51, 95-122
  demographics and composition of,
  7-8, 13-15, 14 (table), 31-34,
  32 (table)
  family education for, 52, 95-122
  family rights litigation in
  New York City, 177-184
  funding of programs for, by level
  of government, 24, 27 (fig.), 28
  growth in population of, 2-3, 15-23,
  29, 30 (fig.)
  health care for, 33, 125-127, 138-139
  percent with experience living
  independently, 155, 156 (fig.)
  public policy for, 23-28, 34-41,
  125-126
  substance abuse among, 33, 127-
  129, 128 (fig.), 148 (fig.)
  undereducation of, 95-97, 100
  See also Children, homeless;
  Parents, homeless
Homeless Family Rights Project, 5, 177
Homeless Rehousing Assistance
  Program (HRAP), New York State,
  157
Homelessness
  definitional parameters of, 171-173
  education, as key to overcoming,
  57-93
  in New York City, 28-41
  reasons for, 13-23, 40-41, 43-44
  return to, after shelter vs. after RET

center, 44-45, 47, 48 (fig.), 154-155
Homelessness assistance programs,
  24-48, 27 (fig.)
  funding by level of government,
  24, 27 (fig.), 28
  reorientation of policy, 43-44
Homes for the Homeless (HFH), 29
  data collection system, 54, 175-176
  educational programs of, 51-52,
  68-70, 74-78, 87-92
  family and adult education
  programs, 100-122
  family preservation programs, 53,
  137-150
  founding of, 7-8
  health care programs, 52, 138
  job training programs, 95-97, 100,
  110-120, 111 (table)
  as a model for homelessness
  assistance programs, 29
  post-shelter support programs, 53,
  157-167
  See also Residential Educational
  Training (RET) centers
Housing
  Housing Workshops (HFH), 157,
  158-159
  public policy for, 154
  transitional housing facilities, 29,
  37, 101
  types of, in New York City, 34-41,
  36 (fig.)
  See also Permanent housing
  programs; Shelter system
Housing and Urban Development
  (HUD), Department of,
  budget spending for housing
  assistance, 16 (fig.), 17
Housing assistance
  federal spending for, 16 (fig.), 17
  public policy, 154
  state and local spending for, 28

In Re Chadbourne Industries Ltd., 183
In Re New York International Hostel,
  Inc., 183

In Re Pan Trading Corp, 183
Independent living skills, 52
  workshops for, 106-110, 115
Intergenerational programs, 75

Jackson v. Grinker, 182
Job internships, 115
Job placement, 116-117
Job training, of homeless parents, 52,
  95-97, 100, 110-120, 111 (table)
Jobs
  low-paying, 97
  unskilled, disappearance of, 96-97
Johnson, Lyndon, 173
Jump-Start Programs (HFH), 51, 70-75
  results of, 83, 86 (fig.)

Koch, Mayor Edward, 5, 7

Lamboy v. Gross, 180
Legal Aid Society, 5, 177
LEGO-logo computer program, 78
Levin, Henry, 75
Literacy programs, 75, 100
Local government, homelessness
  assistance programs, 24-28, 27 (fig.)

McCain v. Dinkins, 180
McCain v. Koch, 177-180
McKinney Act. See Stewart B.
  McKinney Homelessness
  Assistance Act
Mental health problems,
  of homeless children, 126-127
Morton, Rev. James Parks, 6-7

Needs assessment, at RET centers, 51
New York City
  demographic profile of homeless
  children in, 59 (table)
  Department of Cultural Affairs, 82
  Emergency Assistance Units, 5-6
  family rights litigation in, history of,
  177-184
  homelessness in, 28-41
  numbers of homeless in, 2-3, 29,

  30 (fig.)
  post-shelter programs, 157
  public policy for the homeless, 34-41
  shelter system, 2-4, 29, 34-37,
  44-45, 46 (table), 48 (fig.), 157
  spending for the homeless, 34,
  35 (fig.)
  Tier I emergency facilities in, 37
  Tier II transitional facilities in, 37
  types of housing for the homeless,
  34-41, 36 (fig.)
  welfare hotels in, 34-37
New York State, Homeless Rehousing
  Assistance Program (HRAP), 157

O'Donovan v. Dinkins, 184
Omnibus Budget Reconciliation Act
  of 1981, 17

Parents, homeless
  childhood histories of, 131 (table)
  domestic violence among, 33, 129
  educational needs of, 95-122
  involvement in children's
  education programs, 74, 97
  job training of, 95-97, 100, 110-120,
  111 (table)
  profile of those with foster care
  histories, 136 (table)
Permanent housing programs,
  153-168
  placement assistance, 159-162,
  160 (fig.)
  post-placement follow-up, 162-168
  workshops, 158-159
PLUS (Practical Living/Useful Skills)
  program (HFH), 52, 106-110
  results of, 121
  workshops, 115, 157, 158-159
PLUS INC (Practical Living/Useful
  Skills In New Communities)
  (HFH), 53, 158, 162-168
  increasing need for, 163, 166 (fig.)
  results of, 167-168
Poverty
  in America, 11-28

anti-poverty programs, dismantling of, 15-23
breaking the cycle of, 101, 172
education as key to ending, 57-93
link with foster care, 134-135
rates of, in children, 11-13, 12 (fig.)
as root cause of homelessness, 43-44
of single-female families, 17, 18 (fig.)
Pre-school
  programs at RET centers, 51, 70-75
  rates of enrollment by family income level, 71 (fig.)
Prenatal care, 138
Prospect RET center, 50, 75, 139-143
Public policy
  for the homeless, 23-28, 34-41
  for adult literacy, 100
  failure in addressing homelessness, 172-173
  for housing, 154
  for job training of homeless, 100
  for mental and physical health of homeless, 125-126
  for post-shelter support, 155-157

Reagan, Ronald, 15, 17, 29
Recreation programs at RET centers, 51, 78-83, 92-93
Residential Educational Training (RET) centers of HFH, 43-54
  Adult Education Centers, 102-106
  afterschool programs, 51
  compared to shelter system in New York City, 41, 46 (table), 48 (fig.)
  counseling at, 52
  educational programs, 51-52, 68-70, 74-78, 87-92
  funding mechanisms, 185-186
  health care programs, 33, 125-127, 138-139
  intake procedure, 51
  as model of homelessness assistance, 29, 171-173
  needs assessment procedure, 51
  New York City locations, 50

operations of, 50
overview of programs, 49 (chart), 51-54
pre-school programs, 51, 70-75
recreational programs, 51, 78-83, 92-93
See also Homes for the Homeless (HFH)
Roberto Clemente Housing Project, Bronx, 3-4

St. John the Divine, Cathedral of, 6-7
Saratoga RET center, 50
Shelter system
  compared to RET Centers, 41, 46 (table), 48 (fig.)
  living conditions in, 2-4
  in New York City, 29, 34-37, 44-45
  percent of shelters offering educational services, 66, 67 (fig.)
  problems of, 44-45
  recidivism in, 154-155
  types of facilities, 34-41, 36 (fig.)
Single homeless adults, 17, 24, 29
Slade v. Koch, 181
Social programs, federal spending for, 17-20, 19 (fig.)
Social well-being, 20
  index of, 22 (fig.)
State government, homelessness assistance programs, 24-28, 27 (fig.)
Staten Island RET center, 50, 138
Stern, Leonard N., 1-8
Stewart B. McKinney Homelessness Assistance Act, 23-26, 68, 155
  allocation of funds, 23-24, 25 (fig.)
  authorized vs. appropriated funds, 24, 26 (fig.)
Substance abuse
  among the homeless, 33, 127-129, 128 (fig.)
  homeless heads-of-household receiving treatment for, 148 (fig.)
  prevention and intervention programs at RET centers, 53, 146-149

Texas, 68
Tier I emergency facilities,
    in New York City, 37
Tier II transitional facilities,
    in New York City, 37
Together In Emotional Strength
    (TIES) (HFH), 53, 137-138, 146-149
    costs of, vs. foster care, 150
    results, 149
Together In Learning (HFH), 75
Train and Gain (TAG) (HFH), 52,
    114-120
    results, 122
Transitional housing facilities, 29
    benefits of, 101
    Tier II, in New York City, 37

Underclass, 23

Welfare hotels, in New York City,
    34-37
Work. See Jobs